THE Keto SHEET PAN COOKBOOK

THE Keto
SHEET PAN
COOKBOOK

Super Easy Dinners, Desserts, and More!

SARAH ANNE JONES

Photos by Abigail Gehring

Skyhorse Publishing

Skyhorse Publishing books may be purchased in bulk at special discounts for sales promotion, corporate gifts, fund-raising, or educational purposes. Special editions can also be created to specifications. For details, contact the Special Sales Department, Skyhorse Publishing, 307 West 36th Street, 11th Floor, New York, NY 10018 or info@skyhorsepublishing.com.

Skyhorse® and Skyhorse Publishing® are registered trademarks of Skyhorse Publishing, Inc.®, a Delaware corporation.

Visit our website at www.skyhorsepublishing.com.

10 9 8 7 6 5 4 3 2

Library of Congress Cataloging-in-Publication Data is available on file.

Cover design and photo by Abigail Gehring. Recipe for cover photo appears on page 20.

Print ISBN: 978-1-5107-4982-5
Ebook ISBN: 978-1-5107-4983-2

Printed in China

Contents

Introduction

Hi, my name is Sarah and I am a sugar addict.

I know there are millions of people who can say the same. But when I say "sugar addict," I mean that there was a time a few years ago that I realized I never, *ever* went a day without some form of chocolate. That wouldn't be so terrible, but it became more of a habit than anything; "It's the end of the day, I need a treat" kind of thing. And doing that when you know you don't feel good about yourself, and that the behavior is contributing to those negative feelings, is not healthy.

I'm sure many can also relate to the lifelong struggle I have had with my weight. I have tried many different diets, some healthy and some not. Most of them worked, for a while; I feel as if I've lost and gained the same fifty pounds over and over in the past twenty-five years.

Then I had three kids. The weight did not come off very easily anymore, not to mention that the stress of being a mother to three, then a *single* mother to three, made it difficult to focus on myself. I ate merely to survive, and I felt terrible and uncomfortable in my skin.

I have been a member of an online community of moms for about ten years—since I was pregnant with my oldest. It was through this online community that I discovered keto. For a while I would see the discussions and ignore them, because it seemed like a fad and, truly, I wasn't in a mental place to think about changing anything.

One day I wandered into this group online and started reading. At first, it was really overwhelming; there are a lot of terms that experienced keto enthusiasts throw around that don't initially make sense to most people. But it did seem pretty simple overall: just don't eat sugar and grains. There were some handy online lists of foods I *could* eat, which were amazingly helpful.

The first day, I had some bacon with my breakfast, and I realized that focusing on the foods I could eat was probably going to save me, at least until the sugar cravings went away.

I lost thirty-five pounds in the first two and a half months of eating keto, and I had more energy and mental clarity than I had had in a long time. I could go a lot longer without eating—I often skipped breakfast because I just didn't feel like having any. These are all normal side effects of cutting unnecessary carbs out of your life.

I will not say that keto is for everyone—if there's one thing I have learned in my nearly four decades on this planet it's that there are very few things you can make truthful generalizations about. What I will say is that, for me, with my lifetime of unhealthy eating and bingeing, and a family history full of diabetes, I truly believe this is the best way for me to eat. Probably the most recognizable health change is that, in two years of mostly eating keto, I went from having high cholesterol to having normal cholesterol levels.

THE BASICS

So what is keto?

I have to assume, if you picked up this book, you have a passing knowledge of what keto is. Plus, it is continuing to gain in popularity.

The problem is, a lot of the "hype" going on around keto has also created a lot of misconceptions. No, people I know who eat keto do not drink bacon fat for breakfast. I, personally, and a lot of the other people I know who are eating this way, eat far more vegetables than we used to eat.

There are also two different fields of thought about how to eat keto (okay, probably more than two, but two main ones, anyway). What seems to be more dominant is the "high fat" way of doing it. I think this is probably where a lot of the controversy comes from, since we've all been taught that we need to reduce fat in our diets, and that eating too much of it is very, very bad. This "high fat" version of keto is commonly called "medical keto" because it was originated as a diet that was utilized to reduce symptoms in such conditions as epilepsy.

The other field of thought is referred to as "nutritional keto", and that is the version I have been following. This version focuses on high protein, moderate fat, and low carb. The idea is that you stay full and keep your muscles healthy by eating a high level of protein each day, you eat at most 20–25 grams of carbohydrates each day, and you eat a moderate amount of fat. This is the site I would recommend to calculate your macros (protein/fat/carbs): http://lowcarbshow.com/wp-content/uploads/2015/01/chart.jpg

Because it can be so complicated in the beginning, it is usually best, at least for the first two weeks, to just focus on eating no more than 20–25 grams of carbohydrates each day, and eating only the foods considered "ketogenic" foods. Those are:

Meat, most veggies (those that grow aboveground and are green are good rules of thumb), full-fat dairy products (sour cream, *real* butter, both half-and-half and heavy cream, cheese in all forms, etc.), eggs, nuts (walnuts, pecans, almonds, and macadamia nuts), nut butters, and good fats (avocado and avocado oil, coconut oil, and olive oil).

Artificial sugars will vary from person to person, based on preference and how they affect you, specifically. Some choose to use stevia or Splenda, and some avoid them completely. They do tend to create cravings for more sweet things.

A great website to refer to for this information is: https://www.ruled.me/ketogenic -diet-food-list.

Another thing to be aware of early on is supplementing three key elements: salt, magnesium, and potassium. If you do not pay close attention to those, you can start to experience what is commonly referred to as the "keto flu." When your body is adjusting to the new diet, your body can freak out a bit. Keto is a natural diuretic, and it begins to flush your kidneys. You *need* salt, potassium, and magnesium. Don't drink excessive water at the beginning (drink to thirst, don't drown your body). Keto flu is usually a feeling of headaches, extreme fatigue, and just general crappiness. Most people feel it for a few days, starting around day four. You do *not* have to suffer, though. I feel like I have noticed this left out of a lot of keto groups when speaking to newcomers, and it really is important. It's an electrolyte imbalance. Drink some broth. Boil a boullion cube, a packet from the ramen package, pickle juice out of the jar, anything super salty. Salt is the most important electrolyte here. It regulates the other two. Potassium is best gotten from food, like pork, avocado, spinach and dark leafy greens, or walnuts. Magnesium is in food, but most people find a supplement is best. Magnesium malate is typically the version that is most easily absorbed.

For more details on all of these elements and more, please visit: https://www.reddit.com/r /ketogains/wiki/index#wiki_macronutrients.3A_timing.2C_quality_for_keto_and_sports.

KETOSIS VS FAT ADAPTED

"Ketosis" happens when you consume 20 net carbs daily for 3–4 days; it means your body is excreting ketones in your urine. Many people think they need to buy those test strips, but they really aren't necessary. If you are eating that maximum of carbs daily, you *will* be in ketosis. However, if you are motivated by those types of things, feel free to use the strips.

"Fat adapted" is when your body becomes used to utilizing fat as a fuel source instead of carbs, which happens after about 4–6 weeks of consistently eating keto. One of the nice things about being fat adapted is that if you do exceed your carbs one day and happen to knock yourself our of ketosis, it is fairly easy to get back into it because your body is used to it.

It is important to know that just being in ketosis does not guarantee you will lose weight. You do still need to have a caloric deficit in order to lose weight. However, ketosis and fat adaptation make it easier because you are not as hungry and can maintain that caloric deficit without feeling deprived.

For more information about both:

https://www.marksdailyapple.com/what-does-it-mean-to-be-fat-adapted/

https://www.reddit.com/r/keto/comments/a7tfhx/ketosis_vs_fat_adapted/

INTERMITTENT FASTING

Part of eating keto, as I mentioned before, is that your appetite will naturally, over time, decrease. Without the constant up-and-down spikes of carbohydrate intake, your blood sugar will remain steady and you will no longer experience "hanger." As a result, it can be helpful to reduce your eating times to a window of six hours or so, which has shown healthy benefits. This is called intermittent fasting.

Intermittent fasting has obvious benefits when it comes to weight loss; by only eating within a limited window of time, it is easier to keep your calories at a certain level and not exceed them. I will say that, in 2.5 years of eating keto, I haven't done a lot of consistent fasting. Psychologically it has felt too much like restriction to the point of deprivation, so it was hard for me to not feel like it was disordered eating. That felt counterintuitive, because one of the things I gained from changing my way of eating to keto was that it reinvented my relationship with food to one that was healthier.

However, I recently started fasting kind of by chance. I had eaten a late lunch/early dinner at around 4 p.m., and then really was just not hungry again that evening. This ended up being great, because trying to make sure all four of us were fed at dinnertime on any given night can be pretty frustrating. Not having to worry about myself allowed me to focus on the needier members of my family. I also usually have a hard time skipping breakfast, for whatever reason. Not eating at night ends up being easier for me than trying to fast in the morning until lunch.

So I did that one night, then another, and another. It feels like an accomplishment to me, since for a lot of my life my eating has felt out of my control, so being able to eat within a reasonable caloric intake level without feeling deprived has been pretty amazing. For instance, I did Weight Watchers about six years ago, and actually lost about 65 pounds on it. I ended up gaining it all back when I got pregnant with my daughter, though. While doing Weight Watchers was fine, I always ended up feeling hungry without having any "points" left for me to eat.

The other thing I will say about that is that, if you're hungry, eat! There is no need to fast if you don't feel like it. I would say this in particular if you have a history of

disordered eating. Some days you may find yourself hungrier than normal, so eat some food!

For more information on the benefits of intermittent fasting, you can go to this site: https://www.healthline.com/nutrition/what-is-intermittent-fasting.

MY TIPS:

- Use the Meal Planning Pages (page 123–138) to help keep yourself on track. Charting out a week's worth of meals will also make grocery shopping easier and more economical.

- I would suggest you focus on real, whole foods in the beginning. Though there may be desserts in this cookbook, when you're trying to beat the sugar addiction, it can be hazardous to eat "replacement" treats, as they can create more cravings, keeping you in the sweets loop for longer. Try to stick to this for about two weeks. Once you feel really comfortable with the process, I think it's easier to then "play" with what you're eating.

- Different sweeteners have a different impact on each person. For some people, sucralose/Splenda can spike blood sugar, even causing a significant weight loss stall. I like to use erythritol because it does not spike blood sugar, and to me also tastes better than some of the other options.

- In nearly every recipe, I indicate "salt and pepper, to taste." I like salt. A lot. So, when I salt things, it might be considered a little more excessive than others might do. That having been said, I think too many people under-salt their food, when salt is great for bringing out the natural flavors in real food.

- The other thing about salt is that there is so much to the world besides table salt. Himalayan pink salt, sea salt, kosher salt—try some! You'll start to notice how each salt tastes a little different. I personally prefer coarse sea salt for most of my recipes. But, again, use whatever you like best.

- Some of the ingredients commonly used as alternatives in keto—such as almond flour—are best purchased at a big box store, such as Costco or BJ's. A 14-ounce bag at my local grocery store is $7.50, whereas I can get a 3-pound bag at Costco for $13.00. Between that and the bacon, it's definitely worth it to check out the money you can save.

- Exercise is the best way to tone! As a very wise person once said: Keto will make you look good, exercise + keto will make you look good naked! Building muscle is also the best way to burn more calories. Many of the people I speak to about keto do not add their exercise calories into their nutrition tracker. That is entirely your choice, but if you do count them in and suddenly find you're not seeing the results you would like to see, try not eating back your exercise calories for a few weeks and see if that helps. Another important note is that, if you are exercising even moderately, you will need to supplement with more salt to keep your electrolytes in balance.

- Your tastes will change, so don't be afraid to try new foods. Once you've gotten rid of your sugar cravings, you will find that many foods taste different, often much better than they used to. I never would have though I would eat roasted broccoli several times a week, but I do! It's absolutely one of my favorite things to eat! While working on this cookbook, even, I tried new vegetables I really hadn't enjoyed before, such as turnips, radishes, and kale, and they are delicious!

- Sheet pans: I ordered two different rimmed sheet pans from Amazon for the purposes of this cookbook: a 13x18-inch, and a 9x13-inch. I like rimmed over non-rimmed for most of these recipes because I feel it keeps the ingredients and/or any corresponding liquids better contained, but there's certainly no rule saying you can't use whatever cookie sheet you have at home. The smaller sheet pan is better for your pizzas and desserts, unless you are cooking for a large crowd; the larger sheet pan is better for your meat/protein and vegetable meals.

- Lining: you can use parchment paper on the sheet pan, spray with a nonstick cooking spray, or lightly coat with oil. I personally do not particularly like parchment paper because it never quite fits correctly, and the perfectionist in me really hates that. But it does make cleanup easier!

Nutritional Disclaimer: I am not a medical professional. I have spoken with my doctor about eating this way and got her approval before doing it. It is always recommended to seek medical guidance when pursuing a new diet/exercise regimen.

BREAKFAST

Egg, Kale, and Bacon Hash

PREP TIME: 5 minutes
TOTAL TIME: 37 minutes
COOK TIME: 32 minutes
YIELD: 6 servings

(I love eggs, bacon, and home fried potatoes. Radishes make a great replacement for potatoes and are keto-approved! This makes a delicious, quick dinner, too.)

INGREDIENTS:

1 bunch radishes, trimmed and halved

3 cups chopped kale

1 tablespoon olive oil

Sea salt and pepper to taste

½ large onion, diced

8 slices bacon, cut into pieces

3 cloves garlic, minced

6 large eggs

¼ cup crumbled goat cheese

INSTRUCTIONS:

1. Preheat oven to 425°F.
2. Prepare a rimmed 13x18-inch sheet pan by lining with parchment paper or coating with nonstick cooking spray.
3. Arrange radishes and kale on sheet pan in a single layer. Drizzle with olive oil and sprinkle with salt and pepper.
4. Sprinkle onion over the kale and radishes, then place bacon pieces evenly on top.
5. Roast for 15 minutes. Sprinkle with garlic and stir gently.
6. Roast 10 more minutes or until bacon is crisp and veggies are fork-tender. Remove from oven.
7. Make small spaces in the "hash" for each egg. Crack them one at a time into each space, careful to keep the yolk intact. Sprinkle salt and pepper over the eggs.
8. Return the sheet pan to oven and roast for an additional 5–10 minutes or until eggs are set.
9. Remove from oven. Top with crumbled goat cheese.

Nutrition per serving: Calories: 167; Total Fat: 12g; Net Carbs: 5g; Protein: 11g

Eggs in Zucchini Nests

PREP TIME: 10 minutes
TOTAL TIME: 45 minutes
COOK TIME: 35 minutes
YIELD: 4 servings

(You will be the envy of everyone at the office when they smell you reheating this for breakfast! These are easy to pop into the toaster oven on a busy morning for a filling and tasty meal to start your day!)

INGREDIENTS:

4 cups zucchini, peeled, grated

2 tablespoons butter, melted

¼ cup diced onion

½ teaspoon salt, plus more to taste

½ teaspoon pepper, plus more to taste

½ teaspoon paprika

½ teaspoon garlic salt

4 large eggs

¼ cup shredded cheese (I like cheddar)

INSTRUCTIONS:

1. Preheat oven to 400°F. Prepare a rimmed 13x18-inch sheet pan by lining with parchment paper or nonstick cooking spray.
2. Wrap grated zucchini in a cheesecloth or dry towel and squeeze over sink to release excess moisture.
3. In a large bowl, combine zucchini, melted butter, diced onion, salt, pepper, paprika, and garlic salt, until well combined.
4. Spread zucchini mixture in a thin layer on the sheet pan.
5. Bake 20–25 minutes, or until edges begin to turn brown.
6. Remove from oven. Scoop the hash browns into 4 equal mounds, with wells in the middle. Gently crack an egg into each mound, careful to keep the yolk intact.
7. Sprinkle with cheese and season with salt and pepper.
8. Bake an additional 10 minutes, or until eggs are set.

Nutrition per serving: Calories: 207; Total Fat: 16g; Net Carbs: 6g; Total Protein: 10g

Chayote Squash Faux Apple Crisp

PREP TIME: 35 minutes
TOTAL TIME: 75 minutes
COOK TIME: 40 minutes
YIELD: 12 servings

(If you're like me, fall is the time for apple treats! Your craving will be satisfied with this amazing Faux Apple Crisp made with chayote squash. If you cannot find chayote, you can use zucchini instead.)

INGREDIENTS:

Filling:

6 chayote squash

1 cup sugar substitute

½ cup lemon juice

1 tablespoon cinnamon

½ teaspoon nutmeg

3 tablespoons butter, cold, cut into small pieces

Topping:

1¾ cups almond flour

1¼ cup almonds, chopped

1¼ cup pecans, chopped

7 tablespoons sugar substitute

3 teaspoons cinnamon

1 teaspoon vanilla

¼ teaspoon salt

⅓ cup butter, cold, cut into small pieces

INSTRUCTIONS:

1. Place chayote in a large saucepan; add enough water to cover the squash and turn heat to high.
2. Boil for 25–30 minutes. Remove from heat and drain. Allow to cool.
3. Meanwhile, prepare a 9x13-inch sheet pan by lining with parchment paper or coating with nonstick cooking spray.
4. Once squash is cooled, peel and slice into ¼ inch slices.
5. Preheat oven to 350°F.
6. In a medium bowl, combine chayote slices, sugar substitute, lemon juice, cinnamon, and nutmeg.
7. Spread the filling on the sheet pan. Place pieces of butter on top of the filling.
8. Bake the filling for 45 minutes, stirring every 15 minutes.
9. While the squash is baking, make the topping. In a medium bowl, whisk together all of the topping ingredients, except for the butter. Once combined, add the butter and mix using either your fingers or a fork. The mixture should be crumbly.
10. When the squash has been in the oven for 45 minutes, add the crisp topping and return to oven for another 20 minutes, or until topping is golden brown and the squash is fork-tender.

NOTE: If using zucchini instead of chayote, you will need 10 medium zucchini, and you can skip the boiling portion of the recipe.

Nutrition per serving: Calories: 279; Total Fat: 25g; Net Carbs: 8g; Protein: 6g

Frittata with Tomatoes and Ricotta

PREP TIME: 5 minutes
TOTAL TIME: 15 minutes
COOK TIME: 10 minutes
YIELD: 12 servings

This dish is a great way to impress your friends at your next brunch gathering. Or, make it for yourself on Sunday and have breakfast set for the week!

INGREDIENTS:

2 tablespoons olive oil

¼ cup red onion, diced

2 cups Brussels sprouts, shaved

Salt and pepper, to taste

2 cups cherry tomatoes, halved

4 garlic cloves, minced

12 eggs

4 egg whites

½ cup Parmesan cheese, grated

¼ cup heavy cream

1 cup whole milk ricotta cheese

3 teaspoons basil, chopped

Keto Coffee Tip: Many of us were drinking our coffee with a ton of sugar added before we did keto. What some of us discovered is that we loved the creamer more than the coffee. But no worries, there are options: heavy whipping cream with an artificial sweetener, or, better yet, a flavored sugar-free syrup such as is made by Torani. Or almond milk—I use the unsweetened chocolate kind in mine. It's definitely different, but I promise most people either get used to it, or discover they actually enjoy their coffee black!

INSTRUCTIONS:

1. Preheat oven to 425°F. Prepare a rimmed 9x13-inch sheet pan by lining with parchment paper or coating with nonstick cooking spray.
2. In a medium skillet, heat the olive oil on medium-high heat. Add the onion and sauté for 1 minute, stirring. Add Brussels sprouts and season with salt and pepper. Cook, stirring occasionally, for 2 minutes. Add tomatoes and garlic, and sauté another 2–3 minutes.
3. Add vegetable mixture to bottom of sheet pan, distributed evenly.
4. In a large bowl, whisk together eggs, egg whites, Parmesan, and heavy cream, and add salt and pepper to taste. Pour into sheet pan, on top of vegetable mixture.
5. Spoon ricotta on top of eggs, distributing evenly so that a portion will be included in each serving.
6. Bake for 10–15 minutes or until set in the middle. Top with chopped basil.

Nutrition per serving: Calories: 183; Total Fat: 13g; Net Carbs: 3g; Protein: 12g

Sheet Pan Pancakes

PREP TIME: 10 minutes
TOTAL TIME: 40 minutes
COOK TIME: 20–30 minutes
YIELD: 6 servings

I have three kids, and boy, do they love pancakes! I do *not* love them, because they are so much work to make. These sheet pan pancakes are the perfect solution, and are also much healthier than traditional pancakes! If you have people with different preferences—two of my kids like chocolate chips, one does not—you can easily adapt this for each and every person. You can also easily double this recipe for a 13x18-inch pan.

INGREDIENTS:

8 large eggs, separated

1 cup almond flour

4 tablespoons coconut flour

¾ teaspoon salt

4 tablespoons butter, melted

¾ cup heavy whipping cream

3 tablespoons almond butter

1½ teaspoons lemon juice

¼ cup sugar substitute

1 teaspoon orange extract or zest

1 teaspoon vanilla

¾ cup blackberries

INSTRUCTIONS:

1. Preheat oven to 350°F.
2. In a large bowl, add egg yolks, almond flour, coconut flour, and salt. Whisk together until all ingredients are incorporated, then add the butter.
3. Add the heavy whipping cream and almond butter and stir until the batter is smooth. Set aside.
4. In a medium bowl, beat the egg whites and lemon juice on high speed until soft peaks form.
5. Add the sugar substitute, orange extract, and vanilla and beat 1–2 minutes more, until peaks are stiff.
6. Add 1 cup of whipped egg whites to batter and stir to combine.
7. Add half of the batter mixture into the egg whites, folding together very carefully. Do this only until just combined; you do not want to over-fold the mixture.
8. Add the rest of the batter into the whites, again folding until just combined.
9. Line a 9x13-inch sheet pan with parchment paper.
10. Pour the batter onto the sheet pan and tap the sides gently so that the batter is evenly distributed.
11. Place the blackberries evenly in rows on top of the batter.
12. Bake for 20 minutes. After 20 minutes, bake for 5 minutes at a time until golden brown and a toothpick inserted comes out clean.

Nutrition per serving: Calories: 392; Total fat: 31g; Carbohydrates (net): 6g; Note: Net Carbs: 6g; Protein: 21g

Blueberry Cinnamon Vanilla Granola

PREP TIME: 5 minutes
TOTAL TIME: 25 minutes
COOK TIME: 20 minutes
YIELD: 8 servings

This granola is great on top of Greek yogurt or in a bowl with unsweetened almond milk. You can add raspberries or strawberries instead of blueberries, or a combination of all three! You can use any size sheet pan for this recipe, as long as you can lay the granola in a single layer.

INGREDIENTS:

½ cup almonds, chopped

½ cup pecans, chopped

½ cup walnuts, chopped

¾ cup flaxseed

¾ cup unsweetened coconut flakes

3 tablespoons hemp hearts/seeds

¼ cup sugar-free pancake syrup

¼ cup smooth almond butter

1 tablespoon cinnamon

1 teaspoon nutmeg

1 teaspoon vanilla extract

¼ cup dried blueberries, divided

INSTRUCTIONS:

1. Preheat the oven to 325°F. Line your sheet pan with parchment paper.
2. In a food processor, pulse the nuts for about 1 minute.
3. In a medium bowl, combine all remaining ingredients, reserving 2 tablespoons of blueberries for later. Mix until the entire mixture is lightly coated.
4. Pour into your prepared sheet pan and press into the sheet pan firmly and evenly.
5. Bake for 20–25 minutes, until browned.
6. Allow to cool completely, approximately 45 minutes. Break into pieces and add the remaining blueberries. Store in an airtight container in a cool, dry place.

Nutrition per serving: Calories: 275; Total Fat: 22g; Net Carbs: 5g; Protein: 8g

Frittata with Bacon and Spinach

PREP TIME: 20 minutes
TOTAL TIME: 35 minutes
COOK TIME: 15 minutes
YIELD: 12 servings

This dish is perfect for a crowd, or to keep on hand for breakfast throughout the week. It reheats perfectly! There are also so many variations you can do for this: shaved Brussels sprouts or chopped asparagus instead of spinach; chopped ham or pancetta instead of bacon; add mushrooms or hot peppers!

INGREDIENTS:

1 dozen eggs

½ cup heavy cream

Salt and pepper, to taste

2 tablespoons olive oil

8 slices bacon, diced and cooked

8 ounces spinach, wilted

2 cups shredded cheese (I like cheddar)

Optional: Crushed red pepper flakes, to taste

INSTRUCTIONS:

1. Preheat oven to 375°F. Line a rimmed 9x13-inch sheet pan with parchment paper or coat with nonstick cooking spray.
2. In a large bowl, beat eggs, cream, salt, and pepper together.
3. Spread the oil on the sheet pan, even if using parchment paper.
4. Arrange bacon and spinach on sheet pan. Sprinkle cheese on top of those ingredients.
5. Carefully pour egg mixture into sheet pan.
6. Bake for 10–15 minutes or until set in the middle.
7. Remove from oven; top with red pepper flakes, if desired.

Nutrition per serving: Calories: 247; Total Fat: 20g: Net Carbs: 2g; Total Protein: 14g

Western Omelet Pizza

PREP TIME: 15 Minutes
TOTAL TIME: 45 minutes
COOK TIME: 30 Minutes
YIELD: 8 servings

(If you are getting tired of eggs for breakfast, you can make this without the eggs and increase the amount of ham or add bacon to keep the protein up.)

INGREDIENTS:

Crust:

2 cups shredded mozzarella

2 tablespoons cream cheese, softened

1½ cups almond flour

1 large egg

1 teaspoon salt

Pinch red pepper flakes

Topping:

8 eggs, scrambled

12 ounces cooked ham, diced

1 medium green bell pepper, sliced thin

1 medium onion, sliced thin

8 ounces cheese (any type), shredded

INSTRUCTIONS:

1. Preheat oven to 425°F. Line a rimmed 9x13-inch sheet pan with parchment paper, or spray with nonstick cooking spray.
2. In a microwave-safe bowl, combine the mozzarella and cream cheese and microwave for 1 minute on high. Remove from microwave and stir to combine. Return to microwave for 30 seconds or until cheese has melted.
3. Stir in almond flour, egg, and spices until combined.
4. Place the dough on a large piece of parchment paper. Place another sheet of parchment paper on top. With a rolling pin, roll out to a 9x13-inch rectangle.
5. Keeping the dough on the parchment paper, transfer to the sheet pan. I found that I had to reshape the dough a bit when I did this, but the sheet pan made it really easy to do.
6. Bake for 10 minutes or until crust is golden brown. Remove from oven and flip crust to the other side.
7. Top the pizza crust with eggs, ham, bell pepper slices, onion slices, and cheese.
8. Return sheet pan to oven for 9–11 minutes, or until cheese is melted.

Nutrition per serving: Calories: 434: Total Fat: 32g; Net Carbs: 5g; Protein: 30g

POULTRY

Prosciutto-Wrapped Chicken with Kale and Radishes

PREP TIME: 15 minutes
TOTAL TIME: 35 minutes
COOK TIME: 20 minutes
YIELD: 4 servings

(This meal takes very little time to put together but tastes like you cooked all day!)

INGREDIENTS:

4 boneless, skinless chicken breasts

Salt and pepper, to taste

8–12 slices prosciutto

5 tablespoons butter, divided

4 cups radishes, halved

2 tablespoons olive oil, divided

4 cups packed kale, chopped

2 cloves garlic, minced

1 tablespoon fresh sage, minced

1 tablespoon lemon juice

¼ cup dry white wine

Lemon wedges, for garnish

INSTRUCTIONS:

1. Preheat oven to 450°F.
2. Place chicken breasts on a cutting board. Sprinkle with salt and pepper.
3. Wrap 2–3 slices prosciutto around chicken, so that breasts are almost completely covered.
4. Place chicken on sheet pan and drizzle with 2 tablespoons melted butter. Place radishes next to chicken in a single layer and drizzle with 1 tablespoon olive oil and sprinkle with salt and pepper to taste.
5. Bake for 10 minutes, then remove from oven. Add kale to sheet pan; drizzle with remaining olive oil and sprinkle with salt and pepper.
6. Bake for an additional 8–10 minutes, or until chicken reaches an internal temperature of 165°F and radishes are tender.
7. In small saucepan, melt the remaining butter, then add garlic, sage, and lemon juice. Sauté over medium-low heat for about 5 minutes; slowly add the white wine and simmer for an additional 5 minutes. Remove from heat.
8. Serve chicken topped with sage-butter sauce and lemon wedges.

Nutrition per serving: Calories: 454; Total Fat: 22g; Net Carbs: 8g; Protein: 53g

Stuffed Peppers

PREP TIME: 20 minutes
TOTAL TIME: 58 minutes
COOK TIME: 28–35 minutes
YIELD: 4 stuffed peppers

(The peppers infuse the ground turkey with so much flavor in this recipe. This will surely become a family favorite!)

INGREDIENTS

4 bell peppers—green, red, yellow, or orange

1 tablespoon olive oil

1 medium onion, diced

3 cloves garlic, minced

1 pound ground turkey

Salt and pepper to taste

1 teaspoon chili powder

2 cups cauliflower, riced

1 cup chicken stock, divided

2 teaspoons tomato paste

1 cup shredded mozzarella cheese, divided

INSTRUCTIONS:

1. Preheat the oven to 350F. Line a rimmed 13x18-inch sheet pan with parchment paper, or coat with nonstick cooking spray.
2. Cut the tops off the peppers and remove the seeds. Keep the tops. Place the peppers on the sheet pan. Set aside.
3. Heat oil in a large skillet. Add onion and cook until translucent, about 3 minutes. Add garlic and cook until softened, about 1 minute.
4. Add ground turkey, salt, pepper, and chili powder. Cook until browned, about 8 minutes.
5. Add cauliflower rice, ½ cup chicken stock, and tomato paste. Stir. Allow to simmer until most of the liquid is absorbed, about 5 minutes. Remove from heat.
6. Put ¼ of the turkey mixture into each pepper, and put the top of the pepper back on.
7. Pour remaining chicken stock into bottom of sheet pan. Cover lightly with aluminum foil. Place carefully into oven.
8. Bake for 20–25 minutes, or until the peppers have slightly wrinkled. Remove from oven.
9. Remove aluminum foil and tops of peppers. Sprinkle ¼ cup of cheese on top of each pepper.
10. Turn oven to "broil."
11. Return peppers to oven for 8–10 minutes, until cheese has melted and become slightly brown.

Nutrition per serving: Calories: 333; Total Fat: 21g; Net Carbs: 7g; Protein; 32g

Jamaican Jerk Chicken and Turnips

PREP TIME: 15 minutes
TOTAL TIME: 40 minutes
COOK TIME: 25 minutes
YIELD: 4 servings

(During a long New England winter, I start to dream of warm, salty beaches in the Caribbean—and this meal takes me there!)

INGREDIENTS:

Marinated Chicken:

1 pound chicken breasts

1 tablespoon dried thyme

1 tablespoon ground allspice

2 tablespoons brown sugar substitute

1 teaspoon salt

1 teaspoon pepper

1 tablespoon garlic salt

1 teaspoon cinnamon

$1/8$ teaspoon cayenne

½ tablespoon soy sauce

½ tablespoon vinegar

½ tablespoon fresh lime juice

Vegetables:

2 cups chopped turnips (trim, peel, and cut into bite-sized pieces)

1 cup chopped bell peppers

1 red onion, chopped

1 zucchini, sliced

INSTRUCTIONS:

1. Place the chicken in a large plastic storage bag. Pour marinade ingredients onto the chicken. Let rest at least 2 hours and as much as 24 hours ahead of cooking.
2. Preheat oven to 425°F. Spray sheet pan with nonstick cooking spray.
3. Place marinated chicken on sheet pan, reserving the marinade.
4. Place turnips in a small bowl, and toss with 2 tablespoons of the marinade. Arrange on the sheet pan around the chicken.
5. Bake for 10 minutes.
6. Place bell peppers, red onion, and zucchini in a small bowl, and toss with 2 tablespoons of the marinade.
7. Remove sheet pan from oven and flip chicken. Add remaining vegetables to the sheet pan around chicken.
8. Bake for 15 more minutes, or until chicken reaches an internal temperature of 165°F.

Nutrition per serving: Calories: 271; Total Fat: 6g; Net Carbs: 9g; Protein: 36g

Parmesan Garlic Chicken with Brussels Sprouts

PREP TIME: 15 minutes

TOTAL TIME: 1 hour

COOK TIME: 25–30 minutes

YIELD: 4 servings

(The thing about Brussels sprouts is, we were all raised to believe they were a disgusting food. But if you cook them correctly, they are delicious!)

INGREDIENTS:

¼ cup + 2 tablespoons olive oil, divided

6 garlic cloves, minced

4 boneless skinless chicken breasts, pounded to 1-inch thickness

¼ cup Parmesan cheese, grated

1 pound Brussels sprouts, trimmed and halved lengthwise

Salt and pepper, to taste

6 slices uncooked bacon, cut into 1-inch pieces

INSTRUCTIONS:

1. Preheat oven to 425°F. Line a 13x18-inch sheet pan with parchment paper or coat with non-stick cooking spray.
2. Heat ¼ cup olive oil and garlic in a small saucepan on medium-low, until garlic starts to brown. Transfer to a small bowl.
3. Using tongs, dip chicken breasts into the garlic-olive oil infusion, then dip into Parmesan until evenly coated. Transfer to sheet pan.
4. In a medium bowl, toss Brussels sprouts with remaining olive oil, salt, and pepper.
5. Lay the Brussels sprouts on the sheet pan in a single layer. Top with bacon pieces.
6. Bake for 25–30 minutes or until chicken is cooked through and Brussels sprouts are tender.

Nutrition per serving: Calories: 467; Total Fat: 30g; Net Carbs: 3g; Protein: 4g

Bruschetta Chicken

PREP TIME: 15 minutes
TOTAL TIME: 30 minutes
COOK TIME: 15 minutes
YIELD: 4 servings

(Very little brings me greater joy than showcasing my homegrown tomatoes in a tasty dish like this Bruschetta Chicken! Even better when you grow your own basil, too!)

INGREDIENTS:

Balsamic Chicken:

¼ cup balsamic vinegar

¼ cup olive oil

½ teaspoon garlic salt

1 tablespoon Italian seasoning

½ teaspoon salt

½ teaspoon ground pepper

4 chicken breasts

1 cup mozzarella, shredded

Bruschetta Topping:

1 pint grape tomatoes, halved (I used a mixture of yellow and red)

2 tablespoons olive oil

2 tablespoons fresh basil, chopped

5 cloves garlic, minced

Salt and pepper, to taste

INSTRUCTIONS:

1. In a medium-sized bowl, combine the marinade ingredients with a whisk. Add the chicken and cover; marinate for at least a couple of hours, or as long as overnight.
2. Preheat oven to 400°F. Coat your 13x18-inch sheet pan with oil or nonstick cooking spray.
3. Place marinated chicken breasts on sheet pan. Bake for 15 minutes.
4. Meanwhile, in a small bowl, combine the tomatoes, olive oil, basil, garlic, and salt and pepper to taste.
5. Remove chicken from oven and top with mozzarella. Return to oven and bake for another 5–10 minutes, or until internal temperature reaches 165°F.
6. Spoon bruschetta mixture evenly onto each chicken breast.

Nutrition per serving: Calories: 369; Total Fat: 26g; Net Carbs: 6g; Protein: 28g

Chicken Cordon Bleu with Asparagus

PREP TIME: 10 minutes
TOTAL TIME: 40 minutes
COOK TIME: 30 minutes
YIELD: 4 servings

(You'll feel like a professional chef when you present this dish to the family. But don't worry—it's a lot simpler to make than you'd think.)

INGREDIENTS:

4 chicken breasts

4 ounces deli ham

4 ounces Swiss cheese

1 tablespoon paprika

½ tablespoon garlic salt

1 teaspoon dried thyme

Salt and pepper, to taste

2 tablespoons olive oil, divided

1 large bunch asparagus

Juice of 1 lemon

Creamy Dijon Sauce:

½ cup white or apple cider vinegar

2 cloves garlic, minced

2 tablespoons Dijon mustard

2 tablespoons sour cream

Salt and pepper, to taste

INSTRUCTIONS:

1. Preheat oven to 350°F. Coat a 13x18-inch sheet pan with parchment paper or nonstick cooking spray.
2. Place the chicken breasts on a cutting board. Cut a pocket into the side of each breast, being careful not to slice all the way through the breast. Place an equal amount of ham and cheese into each breast.
3. In a small bowl, combine the paprika, garlic salt, thyme, salt, and pepper.
4. Drizzle 1 tablespoon olive oil over chicken. Sprinkle seasoning over chicken.
5. Place the chicken on the sheet pan. Lay the asparagus in a single layer, drizzle with remaining olive oil and lemon juice, and add salt and pepper to taste.
6. Bake for 25–30 minutes, or until chicken is cooked through and juices no longer run pink.
7. While chicken and asparagus are baking, make the creamy Dijon sauce: in a small bowl, whisk together all ingredients.
8. Remove sheet pan from oven. Pour creamy Dijon sauce over chicken. Serve.

Nutrition per serving: Calories: 383; Total Fat: 24g; Net Carbs: 7g; Protein: 42g

Buffalo Chicken Thighs with Blue Cheese Cauliflower

PREP TIME: 10 minutes
TOTAL TIME: 35 minutes
COOK TIME: 35 minutes
YIELD: 4 servings

All the flavor of wings without so much mess! If you're not particularly a fan of blue cheese, you could use a milder cheese like feta, or just roast the cauliflower with olive oil, salt, and pepper.

INGREDIENTS:

3 pounds bone-in, skin-on chicken thighs

4 tablespoons olive oil, divided

2 teaspoons garlic salt

1 teaspoon dried parsley

1 teaspoon pepper, divided

½ teaspoon onion powder

1 head cauliflower, quartered and trimmed

1 tablespoon white wine vinegar

1 tablespoon water

¼ teaspoon salt

2 tablespoons crumbled blue cheese

Buffalo Sauce:

½ cup melted butter

½ cup hot sauce

2 tablespoons white vinegar

3 teaspoons Worcestershire sauce

1 teaspoon garlic powder

INSTRUCTIONS:

1. Preheat oven to 400°F. Line a rimmed 13x18-inch sheet pan with parchment paper or coat with nonstick cooking spray.
2. Add chicken to sheet pan. Pat dry with paper towel. Coat with 2 tablespoons oil.
3. In a small bowl, mix together garlic salt, parsley, ¾ teaspoon pepper, and onion powder. Sprinkle on tops and sides of chicken thighs.
4. Add cauliflower to sheet pan. Drizzle with 1 tablespoon olive oil and sprinkle with salt and pepper.
5. Roast for 20 minutes.
6. While roasting, mix together 1 tablespoon oil, vinegar, water, ¼ teaspoon pepper, salt, and blue cheese in a small bowl.
7. Remove pan from oven after 20 minutes. Coat cauliflower with blue cheese mixture.
8. Return pan to oven for 15–20 minutes, or until internal temperature reaches 165°F.
9. Make Buffalo Sauce: Mix together all ingredients for Buffalo Sauce in bowl. Once cooked, toss chicken thighs in Buffalo Sauce.

Nutrition per serving: Calories: 683; Total Fat: 40g; Net Carbs: 6g; Total Protein: 70g

Teriyaki Chicken with Asparagus

PREP TIME: 10 minutes
TOTAL TIME: 30 minutes
COOK TIME: 20 minutes
YIELD: 4 servings

(This recipe is a family favorite. It works especially well on the grill, but that's not always an option, especially during a Vermont winter!)

INGREDIENTS:

¼ cup olive oil

¼ cup soy sauce or coconut aminos

6 cloves garlic, crushed or minced

3 tablespoons no-sugar-added ketchup

1 tablespoon white vinegar

Salt and pepper, to taste

1 pound chicken breasts, pounded to 1-inch thickness

1 bunch asparagus

1 tablespoon olive oil

INSTRUCTIONS:

1. In a medium bowl, whisk together olive oil, soy sauce, garlic, ketchup, vinegar, salt, and pepper. Add the chicken and cover, marinating 2 hours or up to 24 hours.
2. Preheat the oven to 350°F. Line a rimmed 13x18-inch sheet pan with parchment paper or coat with nonstick cooking spray.
3. Place the asparagus on the sheet pan in a single layer. Drizzle with one tablespoon olive oil. Place the chicken on top of the asparagus, also in a single layer.
4. Bake the chicken for 20–25 minutes, or until chicken is no longer pink and juices run clear.

Nutrition per serving: Calories: 318; Total Fat: 18g; Net Carbs: 5g; Protein: 28g

Lemon Butter Chicken with Green Beans

PREP TIME: 10 minutes
TOTAL TIME: 55–60 minutes
COOK TIME: 45–50 minutes
YIELD: 4 servings

This chicken is very moist and delicious. I always love the brightness of lemon with the richness of butter; the flavors pair perfectly with the chicken and green beans in this dish.

INGREDIENTS:

1 lemon, sliced

4 bone-in chicken breasts with skin

2 tablespoons olive oil, divided

Salt and pepper, to taste

¼ cup chicken broth

¼ cup lemon juice

2 cloves garlic, minced

2 tablespoons butter or ghee, melted

½ tablespoon parsley, finely chopped

1 pound green beans, trimmed

INSTRUCTIONS:

1. Preheat oven to 400°F. Line a 13x18-inch sheet pan with parchment paper or coat with non-stick cooking spray.
2. Scatter lemon slices on the sheet pan.
3. Place the chicken breasts on the sheet pan. Drizzle with olive oil and season generously with salt and pepper.
4. In a small bowl, combine the chicken broth, lemon juice, garlic, butter, and parsley.
5. Spoon ⅓ of the mixture onto the chicken breasts.
6. Bake chicken breasts for 25 minutes.
7. Remove sheet pan from oven. Add green beans to sheet pan. Drizzle with olive oil and season with salt and pepper.
8. Spoon another ⅓ of the lemon butter mixture onto the chicken and green beans.
9. Bake for 20–30 minutes, or until chicken reaches an internal temperature of 165°F.
10. Spoon the remaining sauce onto the chicken breast. Turn the oven to broil for 2–4 minutes, or until the chicken is golden brown in color.

Nutrition per serving: Calories: 334; Total Fat: 16g; Net Carbs: 6g; Protein: 25g

Pesto Chicken with Green Beans and Tomatoes

PREP TIME: 15 minutes
TOTAL TIME: 35 minutes
COOK TIME: 20 minutes
YIELD: 4 servings

(Pesto is so rich with flavor, but even more so when you make it yourself. Store-bought pesto cannot compare to this recipe made fresh at home!)

INGREDIENTS:

Pesto:
1½ cups basil leaves
¼ cup pine nuts
¼ cup fresh grated Parmesan cheese
2 cloves garlic, peeled
Salt and pepper, to taste
½ cup olive oil

Chicken and Vegetables:
1½ pounds boneless skinless chicken breast, cut into tenders
1 pound green beans, trimmed
½ pint cherry tomatoes
¼ cup shredded fresh Parmesan cheese

INSTRUCTIONS:

1. Preheat oven to 400°F. Line a rimmed 13x18-inch sheet pan with parchment paper, or coat with nonstick cooking spray.
2. Add the basil leaves, pine nuts, Parmesan, garlic, salt, and pepper to a food processor or blender. Pulse until the ingredients are coarsely chopped.
3. With the machine running, slowly drizzle in the olive oil. Continue running until mixture is combined, pausing to scrape down the sides. Taste and adjust as necessary. Set aside.
4. In a medium bowl, combine the chicken with ¼ of the pesto until chicken is coated. Place on the sheet pan in a single layer.
5. In a clean bowl, combine the green beans with 3 tablespoons pesto. Add to sheet pan in a single layer.
6. Bake for 10 minutes.
7. In the same bowl that was used for the green beans, combine the tomatoes with 1 tablespoon of the pesto.
8. Remove sheet pan from oven. Add tomatoes in a single layer.
9. Bake for an additional 8–12 minutes or until green beans are tender and chicken reaches an internal temperature of 165°F.
10. Remove sheet pan from oven; spoon an additional ¼ of the pesto over the chicken and vegetables.
11. Serve with more pesto, or reserve remaining pesto in an airtight container in the refrigerator for future use for up to 2 weeks.
12. Sprinkle with shredded Parmesan cheese.

Nutrition per serving: Calories: 416; Total Fat: 34g; Net Carbs: 5g; Protein: 26g

Moroccan Chicken

PREP TIME: 20 minutes
TOTAL TIME: 50 minutes
COOK TIME: 30 minutes
YIELD: 4 servings

(I love trying out foods from different cultures. The spices in this recipe are likely to already be on your spice rack, but combined they create an exotic flavor that is so different from standard American fare. Absolutely delicious!)

INGREDIENTS:

1 tablespoon paprika

2 teaspoons cumin

1 teaspoon coriander

1 teaspoon turmeric

1 teaspoon ground ginger

1 teaspoon ground cinnamon

4 cloves garlic, minced

2 tablespoons chili paste

¼ cup olive oil

¼ cup lemon juice and zest

2 lemons, cut into wedges, divided

2½ pounds chicken thighs and drumsticks

1 red onion, sliced

½ fennel bulb, chopped

1 eggplant, chopped into 1-inch pieces

½ cup olives (I used kalamata)

Salt and pepper, to taste

INSTRUCTIONS:

1. Preheat oven to 350°F. Line a rimmed 13x18-inch sheet pan with parchment paper or coat with nonstick cooking spray.
2. In a small bowl, whisk together spices, garlic, chili paste, olive oil, and lemon juice and zest.
3. Place the chicken thighs and drumsticks on a cutting board. Pat dry with paper towel.
4. Rub half of the spice mixture on the chicken. Place chicken on sheet pan.
5. Place vegetables and olives on sheet pan; season with salt and pepper.
6. Pour remaining spice mixture over all ingredients.
7. Add lemon wedges of 1½ lemon to the pan, scattered throughout.
8. Bake for 30 minutes; remove from oven.
9. Squeeze juice of ½ lemon over the pan.

Nutrition per serving: Calories: 164; Total Fat: 8g; Net Carbs: 8g; Protein: 12g

Chicken Parmesan

PREP TIME: 10 minutes
TOTAL TIME: 22–25 minutes
COOK TIME: 12–15 minutes
YIELD: 6 servings

(Cheesy, saucy, meaty—all the things you love about Italian food, right here! Serve over zucchini noodles, and you'll feel like you're at an Italian restaurant!)

INGREDIENTS:

3 ounces pork rinds, finely crushed

¼ cup grated Parmesan cheese

1 teaspoon garlic salt

1 teaspoon Italian seasoning

1 pound boneless skinless chicken breasts (or 3 breasts), pounded to 1-inch thickness, or cut in half lengthwise

2 eggs, beaten

1 cup no-sugar-added tomato sauce

4 ounces mozzarella cheese, sliced

1 bunch fresh basil

INSTRUCTIONS:

1. Preheat oven to 375°F. Line a 13x18-inch sheet pan with parchment paper or coat with nonstick cooking spray.
2. In a medium bowl, combine the pork rinds, Parmesan, garlic salt, and Italian seasoning.
3. Dip each chicken breast in egg, then into the pork rind mixture, making sure to coat the chicken well.
4. Place the chicken on the sheet pan in a single layer.
5. Bake for 8 minutes.
6. Remove from oven. Spoon the tomato sauce evenly onto each chicken breast. Top each with a slice of mozzarella.
7. Return to oven and bake for an additional 10 minutes or until chicken reaches an internal temperature of 165°F.
8. Turn the oven to broil and cook for an additional 2 minutes, or until cheese is golden brown on top.
9. Remove from oven and top with fresh basil. Serve with zucchini noodles, if desired.

Nutrition per serving: Calories: 412; Total Fat: 19g; Net Carbs: 2g; Protein: 54g

Hoisin Chicken

PREP TIME: 20 minutes
TOTAL TIME: 1 hour
COOK TIME: 40 minutes
YIELD: 4 servings

(I kept this recipe on the mild side. If you like your food a little spicier, add more chili sauce until it's hot enough for you.)

INGREDIENTS:

Hoisin Sauce:

4 tablespoons soy sauce or coconut aminos

2 tablespoons nut butter

1½ teaspoon sweetener

1 teaspoon sriracha chili sauce

1 teaspoon sesame oil

1 teaspoon rice vinegar

5 cloves garlic, minced

Chicken and Vegetables:

⅓ cup Hoisin Sauce

⅓ cup soy sauce or coconut aminos

2 tablespoons sriracha chili sauce

1 tablespoon rice vinegar

2 teaspoons sesame oil

2 cloves garlic, minced

½ teaspoon minced fresh ginger

2 pounds chicken thighs

Salt and pepper, to taste

2 cups cauliflower florets

2 tablespoons olive oil, divided

4 heads baby bok choy

1 medium sweet red pepper, chopped

INSTRUCTIONS:

1. Preheat oven to 400°F. Line a rimmed 13x18-inch sheet pan with parchment paper or coat with nonstick cooking spray.
2. In a small bowl, prepare the hoisin sauce by whisking all the sauce ingredients together.
3. In another small bowl, whisk together ⅓ cup of the hoisin sauce, soy sauce, sriracha chili sauce, rice vinegar, sesame oil, garlic, and ginger. Set aside.
4. Place chicken on the sheet pan in a single layer. Season with salt and pepper. Spoon ⅓ of hoisin mixture on top of chicken.
5. Bake 15 minutes. Remove pan from oven and turn chicken. Add cauliflower to pan in a single layer. Drizzle cauliflower and chicken with ⅓ of the hoisin mixture and 1 tablespoon of olive oil.
6. Bake 15 minutes.
7. In a medium bowl, toss bok choy and red pepper with remaining oil, salt, and pepper.
8. Remove pan from oven; add bok choy and pepper in a single layer. Drizzle with 2 tablespoons of hoisin mixture.
9. Bake 10 minutes, or until chicken reaches internal temperature of 170°F.
10. Remove from oven and drizzle with remaining hoisin mixture.

Nutrition per serving: Calories 465; Total Fat: 27g; Net Carbs: 7g; Protein: 47g

Chicken Fajitas

PREP TIME: 10 minutes
TOTAL TIME: 35 minutes
COOK TIME: 25 minutes
YIELD: 6

(Many stores carry a few different options for keto tortillas now, so if you want the full fajita experience, you can have it! Otherwise, enjoy as directed or over cauliflower rice.)

INGREDIENTS:

¼ cup olive oil

2 teaspoons chili powder

1 teaspoon cumin

½ teaspoon garlic salt

½ teaspoon paprika

½ teaspoon salt

½ teaspoon pepper

1 pound boneless skinless chicken breasts, sliced into strips

1 red pepper, sliced

1 green pepper, sliced

1 yellow pepper, sliced

1 red onion, sliced

1 bunch cilantro, chopped

1 lime, cut into wedges

Optional: cheese, sour cream, guacamole or avocado, jalapeño

INSTRUCTIONS:

1. Preheat oven to 400°F. Line a 13x18-inch rimmed sheet pan with parchment paper or coat with nonstick cooking spray.
2. In a small bowl, combine olive oil and spices.
3. Toss together chicken, veggies, and spice mixture on your sheet pan until all are coated with seasoning, then spread into a single layer.
4. Bake for 25 minutes or until chicken is cooked through.
5. Remove from oven. Top with cilantro and squeeze lime wedges over the chicken. Serve with cheese, sour cream, guacamole or avocado, and jalapeño!

Nutrition per serving: Calories: 179; Total Fat: 11g; Net Carbs: 5g; Protein: 16g

Chicken "Crust" Pizza with White Sauce

PREP TIME: 15 minutes
TOTAL TIME: 35 minutes
COOK TIME: 20 minutes
YIELD: 10 slices

(This pizza is not only delicious, it's an excellent way to get in a good chunk of your daily protein!)

INGREDIENTS:

Crust:

2 pounds of ground chicken

2 eggs

½ cup grated Parmesan cheese

1 tablespoon salt

1 teaspoon garlic salt

1 teaspoon pepper

White Sauce:

2 tablespoons butter

½ small onion

4 cloves garlic, minced

½ cup heavy cream

4 tablespoons cream cheese

$1/8$ teaspoon nutmeg

$1/8$ teaspoon dry mustard

Salt and pepper, to taste

Topping:

12 ounces shredded mozzarella cheese

1 cup cherry tomatoes, halved

½ red onion, sliced

4 slices bacon, chopped and cooked

2 tablespoons basil, chopped

Keto tip: Eating meals at restaurants can be a challenge, especially when you're just starting out. It's ideal if you can check out a menu ahead of time so you can plan; however, a salad with a fatty dressing like ranch is usually fine (no croutons, obviously), or a bunless burger, minus the ketchup.

INSTRUCTIONS:

Make the Crust:

1. Preheat oven to 450°F. Line a rimmed 9x13-inch sheet pan with parchment paper, or coat with nonstick cooking spray.
2. In a large bowl, mix ground meat, eggs, Parmesan cheese, and seasonings until thoroughly combined. Press into bottom of prepared sheet pan.
3. Bake for 10 minutes.

Make the White Sauce:

1. In a medium saucepan, melt the butter. Add onion and cook, until softened, about 3 minutes.
2. Stir in the garlic and cook for 1 minute.
3. Add heavy cream, cream cheese, nutmeg, dry mustard, salt, and pepper, and cook on low heat about 5 minutes, stirring constantly, until cream has thickened slightly. Remove from heat.

Make the Pizza:

1. Once meat crust is cooked, remove from oven.
2. Top with white sauce. Sprinkle on mozzarella cheese, tomatoes, red onion, and bacon.
3. Return to oven for 5 minutes, or until cheese is melted.
4. Top with basil.

Nutrition per serving: Calories: 497; Total Fat: 38g; Net Carbs: 2g; Protein: 39g

Garlic Herb Chicken, Green Beans, and Turnips

PREP TIME: 15 minutes
TOTAL TIME: 35 minutes
COOK TIME: 20 minutes
YIELD: 4 servings

(This chicken is rich, flavorful, and incredibly satisfying. Turnips are fall and winter veggies that don't often get the credit they deserve. They make a great substitute for potatoes and are loaded with fiber, vitamins, and minerals.)

INGREDIENTS:

⅓ cup chicken broth or stock

¼ butter, melted

4 cloves garlic, minced

2 teaspoons fresh parsley, chopped

1 teaspoon fresh thyme, chopped

1 teaspoon fresh rosemary, chopped

4 boneless, skinless chicken breasts

½ pound turnips, peeled and cut into 1-inch pieces

Salt and pepper, to taste

1 pound green beans, trimmed

INSTRUCTIONS:

1. Preheat oven to 400°F. Line a rimmed 13x18-inch sheet pan with parchment paper or coat with nonstick cooking spray.
2. In a small bowl, combine chicken broth, butter, garlic, and herbs.
3. Place chicken and turnips on the sheet pan; season with salt and pepper. Pour half of the sauce over the chicken and turnips.
4. Bake for 15 minutes.
5. Remove sheet pan from oven. Flip chicken breasts. Move turnips to make room for green beans. Pour the remaining sauce over the beans and chicken.
6. Bake for an additional 10 minutes, or until chicken reaches an internal temperature of 165°F.
7. Set the oven to broil and leave in the oven for an additional 2–3 minutes, until chicken is golden brown and turnips are fork-tender and crisp on the outside.

Nutrition per serving: Calories: 349; Total Fat 13g; Net Carbs: 8g; Protein: 42g

Honey Mustard Chicken

PREP TIME: 10 minutes
TOTAL TIME: 40 minutes
COOK TIME: 30 minutes
YIELD: 4 servings

(There isn't actually any honey in this recipe, but it will taste like there is! If you like things a little spicier, double the Dijon mustard in the sauce.)

INGREDIENTS:

1½ pounds skin-on, boneless chicken thighs

1 pound radishes, halved

2 tablespoons olive oil, divided

Salt and pepper, to taste

2 tablespoons sour cream

1 tablespoon water

1 tablespoon Dijon mustard

2 teaspoons apple cider vinegar

1 tablespoon sweetener

1 pound broccoli florets

INSTRUCTIONS:

1. Preheat oven to 400°F. Line a rimmed 13x18-inch sheet pan with parchment paper or coat with nonstick cooking spray.
2. Place the chicken skin-side down on the sheet pan; add the radishes in a single layer. Drizzle with 1 tablespoon olive oil; season with salt and pepper.
3. Bake for 15 minutes.
4. In a small bowl, combine sour cream, water, Dijon mustard, vinegar, and sweetener.
5. Remove the sheet pan from oven. Flip the chicken skin-side up. Brush with the sweet mustard sauce.
6. Add the broccoli to the sheet pan in a single layer. Drizzle with 1 tablespoon olive oil, salt, and pepper.
7. Bake for 15 minutes, or until chicken and radishes are crispy on the outside and broccoli is cooked as desired, and chicken reaches an internal temperature of 165°F.

Nutrition per serving: Calories: 364; Total Fat: 27g; Net Carbs: 7g; Protein: 23g

Buffalo Chicken Pizza

PREP TIME: 20 Minutes
TOTAL TIME: 42–45 Minutes
COOK TIME: 22–25 Minutes
YIELD: 8 servings

(This recipe is easy to double and take to a football party so you don't have to feel deprived while everyone else snacks on junk food! In fact, you'll be the star of the party.)

INGREDIENTS:

Crust:
2 cups shredded mozzarella
2 tablespoons cream cheese, softened
1 large egg
1½ cups almond flour
1 teaspoon salt

Buffalo Sauce:
½ cup butter, melted
½ cup hot sauce
2 tablespoons white vinegar
3 teaspoons Worcestershire sauce
1 teaspoon garlic powder

Topping:
1½ pounds boneless skinless chicken breast, cooked, cubed
½ cup shredded cheddar cheese, divided
½ cup shredded mozzarella, divided

INSTRUCTIONS:

1. Preheat the oven to 425°F. Line a rimmed 9x13-inch sheet pan with parchment paper or coat with nonstick cooking spray.
2. Make the Crust: In a microwave-safe bowl, combine the mozzarella and cream cheese and microwave for 1 minute on high. Remove from microwave and stir to combine. Return to microwave for 30 seconds or until cheese has melted.
3. Stir in egg, almond flour, and salt until combined.
4. Place the dough on a large piece of parchment paper. Place another sheet of parchment paper on top. With a rolling pin, roll out to a 9x13-inch rectangle.
5. Keeping the dough on the parchment paper, transfer to the sheet pan. Bake for 10 minutes.
6. Make the Buffalo Sauce: In a small bowl, combine all of the ingredients for the Buffalo Sauce.
7. Make the Pizza: Remove the sheet pan from the oven. Brush with 3 tablespoons of the Buffalo Sauce.
8. In a medium bowl, toss the cubed chicken with the remaining Buffalo Sauce. Add to pizza, and top with cheese.
9. Bake until crust is golden brown and cheese is melted, 12–15 minutes. Serve with celery and blue cheese or ranch dressing.

Nutrition per serving: Calories: 423; Total Fat: 30g; Net Carbs: 3g; Protein: 33g

Red Curry Chicken with Crispy Kale

PREP TIME: 10 Minutes
TOTAL TIME: 1 hour
COOK TIME: 50 minutes
YIELD: 4 servings

(You can ask your butcher to break down a whole chicken for you, or you can do it yourself. Also, if you cannot find the red curry paste at your grocery store, you can substitute sriracha sauce.)

INGREDIENTS:

2 medium rutabaga, peeled and cut into wedges

1 medium red onion, cut into wedges

3 garlic cloves, minced

1 tablespoon freshly grated ginger

3 tablespoons olive oil, divided

Salt and pepper, to taste

2 teaspoons red curry paste

2 tablespoons fresh lemon juice

½ tablespoon sweetener

1 whole chicken, separated into parts

2 cups kale, roughly chopped

INSTRUCTIONS:

1. Preheat the oven to 425°F. Line a rimmed 13x18-inch sheet pan with parchment paper, or coat with nonstick cooking spray.
2. Place the rutabaga, red onion, garlic, and ginger on the sheet pan. Drizzle with 1 tablespoon olive oil and season with salt. Toss to combine and spread out into a single layer.
3. In a small bowl, combine the curry paste, lemon juice, sweetener, 2 tablespoons olive oil, and salt and pepper to taste.
4. Place the pieces of chicken in a single layer on top of the vegetables. Rub the chicken all over with half of the red curry mixture.
5. Bake for 40 minutes, or until chicken starts to turn brown.
6. In a large bowl, toss kale with the remaining curry mixture until fully coated.
7. Remove the sheet pan from the oven and place the kale among the other vegetables. Return the sheet pan to the oven and bake for an additional 10 minutes, or until kale is wilted and chicken reaches an internal temperature of 165°F.
8. If desired, serve with cauliflower rice.

Nutrition per serving: Calories: 395; Total Fat: 26g; Net Carbs: 8g; Protein 22g

Cashew Chicken

PREP TIME: 10 minutes
TOTAL TIME: 26–30 minutes
COOK TIME: 16–20 minutes
YIELD: 4 servings

You'll be sure to impress when placing this dish on the dinner table! In the instructions below you can use whichever nut butter you prefer; peanut butter isn't technically keto, but some people still use it. The most common replacement is almond butter.

INGREDIENTS:

Sauce:

¾ cup soy sauce or coconut aminos

2 teaspoons sriracha chili sauce

1 tablespoon nut butter

1½ tablespoons apple cider vinegar

2 tablespoons sweetener

2 teaspoons sesame oil

1 teaspoon peeled and minced fresh ginger

5 cloves garlic, minced

1 cup water, more or less depending on desired thickness

Pinch xantham gum

Chicken and Vegetables:

4 boneless skinless chicken breasts or thighs, cut into 1-inch cubes

Salt and pepper, to taste

1½ cups broccoli florets

1 red bell pepper, chopped

¼ cup roasted, unsalted cashews

Optional: cauliflower rice

INSTRUCTIONS:

1. Preheat oven to 400°F. Line a rimmed 13x18-inch sheet pan with parchment paper, or coat with nonstick cooking spray.
2. Make the sauce: In a medium saucepan over medium heat, combine the sauce ingredients except for the xantham gum, whisking constantly until simmering. Add xantham gum and stir frequently, until sauce thickens. Set aside.
3. Place the chicken on the sheet pan; season with salt and pepper. Drizzle half of the sauce over the chicken.
4. Bake for 8 minutes.
5. Remove the sheet pan from the oven. Add the broccoli, peppers, and cashews in a single layer around the chicken. Season the vegetables with salt and pepper, then drizzle with ½ of the remaining sauce; toss everything to coat.
6. Bake for an additional 8–10 minutes or until the chicken is cooked through
7. Serve with remaining sauce and cauliflower rice, if desired.

Nutrition per serving: Calories: 302; Total Fat: 14g: Net Carbs: 7g; Protein: 29g

BEEF & PORK

Sheet Pan Tacos

PREP TIME: 15 minutes

TOTAL TIME: 25 minutes

COOK TIME: 10 minutes

YIELD: 8 servings

Taco night gets even easier when you throw everything in a sheet pan! No more dropping everything out of the shell and onto your shirt.

INGREDIENTS:

2½ pounds lean ground beef

1 cup chopped onion

1 tablespoon ground chili powder

1½ teaspoons cumin

1 teaspoon paprika

½ teaspoon garlic salt

¼ teaspoon salt

¼ teaspoon pepper

3 cups shredded cheese

2 avocados, diced

2 jalapeños, diced

1 cup chopped iceberg lettuce

Optional: cilantro, salsa, and sour cream

INSTRUCTIONS:

1. Preheat the oven to 400°F.
2. In a large bowl, mix together the ground beef, onion, and all the seasonings.
3. Line a rimmed 13x18-inch sheet pan with parchment paper or coat with nonstick cooking spray.
4. Spread the meat mixture on the greased sheet pan. Bake for 20 minutes.
5. Remove pan from oven and top meat with cheese. Bake for another 10–20 minutes, or until cheese is melted.
6. Remove from oven. Top with avocado, jalapeños, lettuce, and other toppings as desired.

Nutrition per serving: Calories: 288; Total Fat: 23 g; Net Carbs: 4g; Protein: 15g

Pork Tenderloin with Chili Dijon Glaze

PREP TIME: 15 minutes
TOTAL TIME: 40 minutes
COOK TIME: 25 minutes
YIELD: 6 servings

(For presentation purposes, you could blend the sweet chili sauce in a food processor, blender, or with an immersion blender. The flavors are good either way, but I think it's prettier when it's blended. However, for ease and speed of preparation, I didn't include blending in the instructions below.)

INGREDIENTS:

Spice Rub:

1 tablespoon chili powder

1 tablespoon garlic salt

1 teaspoon salt

1 teaspoon cumin

1 teaspoon onion powder

½ teaspoon paprika

¼ teaspoon pepper

1 tablespoon olive oil

Pork and Vegetables:

1½-pound pork tenderloin, patted dry

1 pound green beans, trimmed

1 cup rutabaga pieces (peel and cut into 1-inch pieces)

2 tablespoons olive oil

Sweet Chili Sauce:

2 red chilies, chopped

1 tablespoon tomato paste

¼ cup sugar substitute

¼ cup rice vinegar

2 cloves garlic, crushed

½ teaspoon ginger, grated

½ teaspoon salt

Chili Dijon Sauce:

1 teaspoon Chili Rub

½ cup Sweet Chili Sauce

¼ cup Dijon mustard

1 teaspoon Worcestershire sauce

INSTRUCTIONS:

1. Preheat oven to 425°F. Line a rimmed 13x18-inch sheet pan with parchment paper or coat with nonstick cooking spray.
2. Make the Spice Rub: In a small bowl, combine all the spices. Reserve 1 teaspoon of the Rub in a separate bowl to be combined with the Chili Dijon Sauce.
3. Combine 3 tablespoons Rub with 1 tablespoon olive oil. Rub all over pork. Set aside.
4. Make the Sweet Chili Sauce: Place all ingredients for chili sauce into saucepan on medium-high heat. Bring to a boil.
5. Reduce to a simmer, stirring frequently for 5 minutes.

6. Remove from heat and allow to cool.
7. Prepare the Vegetables: Place the green beans and rutabaga on the sheet pan. Toss with 2 tablespoons olive oil and 1 teaspoon Spice Rub. Season with salt and pepper, to taste. Spread out to a single layer.
8. Make the Chili Dijon Sauce: In a small bowl, combine 1 teaspoon Spice Rub with the Sweet Chili Sauce, Dijon mustard, and Worcestershire sauce.
9. Lay pork on top of vegetables. Brush with ¼ cup Chili Dijon Sauce.
10. Bake for 25–30 minutes, or until the thickest part of the tenderloin reaches an internal temperature of 145°F.
11. Allow pork to rest for 10 minutes before slicing. Serve with remaining Chili Dijon Sauce.

Nutrition per serving: Calories: 245; Total Fat: 9g; Net Carbs: 8g; Protein: 22g

Stuffed Poblano Peppers

PREP TIME: 15 minutes
TOTAL TIME: 55 minutes
COOK TIME: 40 minutes
YIELD: 8 servings

Prep ground beef in one large batch on the weekend and store in freezer bags. Then it will be ready to go to put these together for your weeknight dinner—you can either thaw overnight or just cook from frozen. Easy-peasy lemon squeezy!

INGREDIENTS:

4 poblano peppers

1 tablespoon olive oil

1 pound lean ground beef

2 tablespoons tomato paste

2 teaspoons chili powder

1 teaspoon cumin

Salt and pepper, to taste

8 ounces cream cheese, softened

1 cup shredded cheese

INSTRUCTIONS:

1. Preheat broiler. Line a 13x18-inch rimmed sheet pan with parchment paper or coat with nonstick cooking spray.
2. Slice each poblano pepper in half lengthwise. Remove seeds.
3. Place peppers cut-side down on the sheet pan and broil about 5 minutes, until skins blister. Remove from oven and turn open-side up. Set aside.
4. Set oven to 400°F.
5. Heat a skillet over medium heat. Add olive oil to pan, then add ground beef and cook until browned.
6. Add tomato paste, chili powder, cumin, salt, and pepper to the ground beef. Cook, stirring, until combined, about 2 minutes. Remove from heat.
7. In a large bowl, combine ground beef mixture and cream cheese.
8. Stuff each pepper with the beef mixture. Add shredded cheese on top.
9. Bake 10 minutes, or until cheese is melted and golden brown.

Nutrition per serving: Calories: 294; Total Fat: 22g; Net Carbs: 5g; Protein: 18g

Ranch Kielbasa and Zucchini

PREP TIME: 10 minutes
TOTAL TIME: 25 minutes
COOK TIME: 15 minutes
YIELD: 4 servings

I started making this in a skillet and used to "cheat" by using a packet of ranch dressing. It was incredibly easy and really, really tasty. However, ranch packets aren't really "keto" (neither are taco packets), so I started making the ranch powder from scratch.

INGREDIENTS:

Ranch Powder:

2 teaspoons lemon zest

2 teaspoons dried parsley

1 teaspoon dried dill

1 teaspoon dried chive

½ teaspoon garlic salt

½ teaspoon onion powder

½ teaspoon salt

¼ teaspoon black pepper

Kielbasa and Veggies:

12-ounce package precooked kielbasa, sliced into ½-inch rounds

1 medium/large zucchini, sliced into 1-inch pieces

1 cup cherry tomatoes

Salt and pepper, to taste

4 ounces goat cheese

INSTRUCTIONS:

1. Preheat oven to 400°F. Line a 13x18-inch rimmed sheet pan with parchment paper or coat with nonstick cooking spray.
2. Make the Ranch Powder: In a small bowl, combine all ingredients with a whisk.
3. In a medium bowl, combine kielbasa, zucchini, and tomatoes. Add 2 tablespoons Ranch Powder and toss to coat.
4. Place kielbasa and vegetables on the sheet pan in a single layer. Add salt and pepper as desired.
5. Bake for 30–45 minutes or until vegetables are tender.
6. Serve with goat cheese.

Nutrition per serving: Calories: 291; Total Fat: 15g; Net Carbs: 6g; Protein: 19g

Bacon-wrapped Mini Meat Loaves with Brussels Sprouts

PREP TIME: 35 minutes
TOTAL TIME: 70–75 minutes
COOK TIME: 35–40 minutes
YIELD: 8 servings

(My super-picky son shocked me one day when he told me he liked meat loaf (he'd tried it at school)! What kid likes meat loaf? Well, all kids will when it's wrapped in bacon and topped with this delicious sauce!)

INGREDIENTS:

1 pound lean ground beef

1 pound ground pork

¼ cup almond flour

¼ cup Parmesan cheese

1 egg

½ small onion, grated

Salt and pepper to taste

8 slices bacon, cut in half

½ cup no-sugar-added ketchup

1 tablespoon brown mustard

½ cup brown sugar substitute

2 cups Brussels sprouts, cut in half lengthwise

1 medium red onion, sliced thinly

6 cloves garlic, sliced

2 tablespoons olive oil

INSTRUCTIONS:

1. Preheat oven to 375°F. Spray your sheet pan with nonstick cooking spray.
2. Mix together meats, almond flour, Parmesan cheese, egg, onion, salt, and pepper.
3. With your hands, form the meat loaf mixture into 8 rectangular loaves, about 2 inches thick, on one side of the sheet pan, leaving room for the Brussels sprouts.
4. Wrap bacon around each loaf, tucking the ends under the sides.
5. Combine ketchup, mustard, and brown sugar substitute in a small bowl. Brush on top of meat loaves.
6. In a bowl, combine the Brussels sprouts, onion, and garlic. Toss with oil, salt, and pepper.
7. Spread Brussels sprouts mixture on sheet pan.
8. Bake for 40 minutes. Change oven setting to "broil" to crisp the bacon.

Nutrition per serving: Calories: 414; Total Fat: 28g; Net Carbs: 8g; Protein: 31g

BLT Pizza with Roasted Garlic Aioli

PREP TIME: 15 minutes
TOTAL TIME: 45 minutes
COOK TIME: 30 minutes
YIELD: 6 servings

(The garlic aioli on this pizza kicks the whole thing up several notches. This recipe is also really easy to double for a 13x18-inch sheet pan if you need to feed a crowd!)

INGREDIENTS:

Crust:

2 cups shredded mozzarella

2 tablespoons cream cheese, softened

1 large egg

1½ cups almond flour

1 teaspoon salt

Pinch red pepper flakes

Garlic Aioli:

¼ cup mayonnaise

4 cloves roasted garlic (see note below)

Salt, to taste

Toppings:

1 cup arugula

6 slices bacon, diced and fried

½ cup cherry tomatoes, halved

INSTRUCTIONS:

1. Preheat oven to 425°F. Line a rimmed 9x13-inch sheet pan with parchment paper or coat with nonstick cooking spray.
2. In a microwave-safe bowl, combine the mozzarella and cream cheese and microwave for 1 minute on high. Remove from microwave and stir to combine. Return to microwave for 30 seconds, or until cheese has melted.
3. Stir in egg, almond flour, and spices until combined.
4. Place the dough on a large piece of parchment paper. Place another sheet of parchment paper on top. With a rolling pin, roll out to a 9x13-inch rectangle.
5. Keeping the dough on the parchment paper, transfer to the sheet pan. I found that I had to reshape the dough a bit when I did this, but the sheet pan made it really easy to do.
6. Bake for 10 minutes, or until crust is golden brown. Remove from oven and flip crust to the other side. Bake for another 10 minutes.
7. Make the Garlic Aioli: In a small bowl, stir together the mayonnaise, roasted garlic, and salt, until well combined.
8. Make the Pizza: Spread the Garlic Aioli on the crust. Top with arugula, bacon, and cherry tomatoes.

Nutrition per serving: Calories: 252; Total Fat: 24g; Net Carbs: 3g; Protein: 9g

Roasted Garlic: Prepare a head of garlic by chopping off the top ½ inch. Place on a large piece of aluminum foil and top with olive oil. Wrap completely in the aluminum foil. Place aluminum foil over the pan. Place in the oven for 20–25 minutes. Remove and set aside.

Ranch Sheet Pan Burgers and "Fries"

PREP TIME: 10 minutes
TOTAL TIME: 25 minutes
COOK TIME: 15 minutes
YIELD: 4 servings

(This meal is one of the easiest ways to satisfy the whole family, keto- and non-keto alike! You can either bake the fries first and then remove from pan, or use two separate sheet pans. It is best to serve the turnip fries immediately after cooking, so, if you can, use two sheet pans.)

INGREDIENTS:

Turnip Fries:

2 cups turnip pieces (peel and cut into ½ inch matchsticks)

2 tablespoons olive oil

Salt and pepper, to taste

Ranch Sheet Pan Burgers:

2 teaspoons lemon zest

2 teaspoons dried parsley

1 teaspoon dried dill

1 teaspoon dried chive

½ teaspoon garlic salt

½ teaspoon onion powder

½ teaspoon salt

¼ teaspoon black pepper

1½ pounds ground beef

6 slices raw bacon, cut in half

1 red onion, sliced into 4 slices

4 slices cheese (I used cheddar)

INSTRUCTIONS:

1. Preheat oven to 425°F. Line two rimmed 13x18-inch sheet pan with parchment paper or coat with nonstick cooking spray.
2. In a medium bowl, toss the turnip fries with olive oil, salt, and pepper.
3. Place in a single layer on a sheet pan. Bake for 25–30 minutes.
4. In a medium bowl, combine spices and ground beef. Form into 4 equal patties and place on sheet pan.
5. Place the bacon and onion slices on the same sheet pan.
6. When turnips have been in the oven for approximately 7 minutes, place the burgers into the oven.
7. Bake for 18 minutes.
8. Remove sheet pans from oven. Set oven to broil.
9. Place 1 slice of cheese on each burger.
10. Return burgers to oven and broil for 2 minutes, or until cheese is melted.

Nutrition per serving: Calories: 383; Total Fat: 33g; Net Carbs: 7g; Protein: 14g

Kielbasa and Cabbage

PREP TIME: 5 minutes
TOTAL TIME: 30 minutes
COOK TIME: 25 minutes
YIELD: 4 servings

(Be careful with buying kielbasa/precooked sausage; the carb counts can be a little on the high side. I have found that beef is usually a little lower in carbs, and I usually stick with Hillshire Farms.)

INGREDIENTS:

3 cloves garlic, minced

2 teaspoons paprika

2 tablespoons olive oil, divided

1 red chili pepper, seeds removed, minced

1 medium green cabbage, sliced thin

12-ounce package precooked sausage (I used kielbasa)

1 medium red onion, diced

INSTRUCTIONS:

1. Preheat oven to 375°F. Line a rimmed 13x18-inch sheet pan with parchment paper or coat with nonstick cooking spray.
2. In a medium bowl, combine garlic, paprika, 1 tablespoon olive oil, and red chili pepper. Add cabbage and toss to coat.
3. Place cabbage, precooked sausage, and onion on the sheet pan in a single layer.
4. Bake for 25 minutes.

Nutrition per serving: Calories: 387; Total Fat: 7g; Net Carbs: 4g; Protein: 11g

Philly Cheesesteak

PREP TIME: 5 minutes
TOTAL TIME: 25 minutes
COOK TIME: 20 minutes
YIELD: 4 servings

(You can use a different cheese, if you prefer. I am emphatically against American cheese (it's *not* cheese!), but if that's what you like, do it!)

INGREDIENTS:

1 pound flank steak, sliced

1 onion, sliced

2 green bell peppers, sliced

8 ounces mushrooms, sliced

3 tablespoons soy sauce or coconut aminos

1 tablespoon olive oil

½ teaspoon salt

½ teaspoon pepper

4 slices provolone

INSTRUCTIONS:

1. Preheat oven to 400°F. Line a rimmed 13x18-inch sheet pan with parchment paper or coat with nonstick cooking spray.
2. Place the steak and vegetables on the sheet pan in a single layer.
3. In a small bowl, combine the soy sauce, olive oil, salt, and pepper. Pour it over the steak and vegetables.
4. Bake for 15 minutes.
5. Remove the sheet pan from the oven. Top the sheet pan with the cheese slices and return to oven. Set the oven to broil and return the pan to the oven for 5 minutes, or until cheese is melted and golden brown

Nutrition per serving: Calories: 351; Total Fat: 20g; Net Carbs: 6g; Protein: 34g

Garlic Herb Pork Tenderloin with Broccoli

PREP TIME: 10 minutes
TOTAL TIME: 25 minutes
COOK TIME: 15 minutes
YIELD: 4 servings

I was surprised when I recently discovered that pork doesn't need to be cooked as thoroughly as we were once told it needed to be. The USDA recommends cooking pork until the internal temperature reaches 145°F. When I took mine out of the oven at 150°F, it was pinker than I am used to, but was incredibly tender.

INGREDIENTS:

1 tablespoon fresh rosemary, minced

2 tablespoons fresh Italian parsley, minced, divided

1 tablespoon fresh basil, minced

1½ pounds pork tenderloin

Salt and pepper, to taste

1 medium head broccoli

1 tablespoon olive oil

¼ cup butter, melted

4 cloves garlic, minced

INSTRUCTIONS:

1. Preheat oven to 425°F. Line a rimmed 13x18-inch sheet pan with parchment paper or coat with nonstick cooking spray.
2. In a small bowl, combine rosemary, 1 tablespoon parsley, and basil.
3. Season all sides of pork tenderloin with herbs, salt, and pepper.
4. Place pork on sheet pan.
5. Add broccoli; drizzle with olive oil and season with salt.
6. Bake for 15 minutes, or until tenderloin reaches an internal temperature of 150°F.
7. Remove from oven and allow to rest for 5 minutes.
8. Whisk together the butter, garlic, and remaining tablespoon of parsley. Pour over pork and broccoli.
9. Slice pork into 1-inch medallions and serve.

Nutrition per serving: Calories: 432; Total Fat: 21g; Net Carbs: 7g; Protein: 49g

Steak Dinner

PREP TIME: 10 minutes
TOTAL TIME: 35 minutes
COOK TIME: 25 minutes
YIELD: 4 servings

If you prefer your steak cooked well done, you may want to check the vegetables and possibly remove them from the sheet pan before the steak is fully cooked so it can broil on its own.

INGREDIENTS:

3 cloves garlic, minced

1 teaspoon paprika

1 teaspoon dried Italian seasoning

1 teaspoon red pepper flakes

Salt and pepper, to taste

2 tablespoons olive oil, divided

1 pound green beans, trimmed

2 cups radishes, quartered

1½ pounds New York strip steak

2–3 tablespoons butter

½ cup Parmesan, grated

INSTRUCTIONS:

1. Preheat oven to 425°F. Line a rimmed 13x18-inch sheet pan with parchment paper or coat with nonstick cooking spray.
2. In a medium bowl, combine garlic, paprika, Italian seasoning, red pepper flakes, salt, pepper, and 1 tablespoon olive oil. Add green beans and radishes and toss to coat.
3. Place vegetables on sheet pan in a single layer. Bake 15 minutes.
4. Remove sheet pan from oven. Move vegetables to make room for steak. Add steak and season with salt and pepper. Drizzle with remaining olive oil and place pats of butter all over the steak.
5. Set oven to broil.
6. Broil for 5 minutes; flip the steaks. Broil for another 5 minutes, or until steaks are to desired doneness.
7. Top vegetables with grated Parmesan. Serve.

Nutrition per serving: Calories: 600; Total Fat: 43g; Net Carbs: 7g; Protein: 42g

Beef and Broccoli

PREP TIME: 10 minutes

TOTAL TIME 30 MINUTES

COOK TIME: 20 minutes

YIELD: 4 servings

If your fridge is as stuffed full as mine, you may have a hard time fitting a bowl in there to marinate the steak. As an alternative, you can use a freezer bag (because of the double seal), which takes up much less space!

INGREDIENTS:

½ cup soy sauce or coconut aminos, divided

2 teaspoons fresh grated ginger, divided

4 cloves garlic, minced

Pinch red pepper flakes

2 tablespoons sesame oil

2 tablespoons rice vinegar

1 pound flank steak, sliced

2½ cups broccoli florets

½ cup beef broth

Salt and pepper, to taste

Sesame seeds for garnish

INSTRUCTIONS:

1. In a medium bowl, combine soy sauce, ginger, garlic, red pepper flakes, sesame oil, and rice vinegar. Add the steak and allow to marinate for at least 1 hour and up to 24 hours.
2. Preheat the oven to 425°F. Line a rimmed 13x18-inch sheet pan with parchment paper or coat with nonstick cooking spray.
3. Remove the steak from the marinade and place in a single layer on the sheet pan.
4. Add the broccoli to the marinade, only long enough to be coated. Add to the sheet pan in a single layer, being careful that the steak and broccoli to do not overlap. Drizzle with beef broth and add salt and pepper to taste.
5. Bake for 12–15 minutes, until steak is cooked to desired doneness and broccoli is fork-tender.
6. Remove from oven and sprinkle with sesame seeds. Serve.

Nutrition per serving: Calories: 289; Total Fat: 16g; Net Carbs: 5g; Protein: 25g

Spaghetti Squash Carbonara

PREP TIME: 10 minutes
TOTAL TIME: 60 minutes
COOK TIME: 50 minutes
YIELD: 4 servings

(At this point in my keto journey, I don't miss many of the carb-laden foods I used to eat. But who doesn't wish for a big bowl of pasta once in a while? This dish will satisfy your craving, I promise.)

INGREDIENTS:

1 large spaghetti squash (3–4 pounds), halved lengthwise and seeds scooped out

1 tablespoon olive oil

Salt and pepper, to taste

8 slices bacon, diced

1 small onion, diced

4 large eggs

¼ cup ricotta cheese

1¼ cups fresh Parmesan cheese, grated, divided

INSTRUCTIONS:

1. Preheat the oven to 375°F. Line a rimmed 13x18-inch sheet pan with parchment paper or spray with nonstick cooking spray.
2. Brush the inside of each squash half with olive oil and season with salt and pepper. Lay halves cut-side down on sheet pan. Bake for 20 minutes.
3. Remove pan from oven. Lay the bacon and onion in a single layer next to the squash. Bake for 15–25 more minutes, or until squash is tender when pierced with a fork.
4. In a medium bowl, whisk the eggs, then whisk in the ricotta.
5. Remove sheet pan from oven. Fold cooked bacon and onion into the eggs, then 1 cup of Parmesan cheese.
6. Shred the inside of the squash with a fork to make spaghetti-like strings; remove from the outer shell.
7. Mix the squash strings into the egg mixture. Replace the parchment paper on the sheet pan with a fresh sheet. Spread the mixture on the pan.
8. Top with remaining Parmesan cheese, salt, and pepper.
9. Bake 10–15 minutes, or until eggs are set.

Nutrition per serving: Calories: 280; Total Fat: 22g; Net Carbs: 3g; Protein: 17g

Steak Tips

PREP TIME: 15 minutes
TOTAL TIME: 43 Minutes
COOK TIME: 28 Minutes
YIELD: 4 servings

(I recommend tripling the steak tips in this for easy meals later in the week; throw them on top of a salad or pair with your favorite cold veggies!)

INSTRUCTIONS:

Marinade:

¼ cup balsamic vinegar

3 cloves garlic

1 tablespoon fresh rosemary, minced

½ teaspoon sea salt

½ teaspoon black pepper

1 teaspoon Dijon mustard

⅓ cup olive oil

Steak and Vegetables:

1 pound sirloin steak tips, 1½-inch pieces

1 red onion, sliced

1 red bell pepper, sliced

1 bunch asparagus, trimmed, cut to 2-inch pieces

1 medium zucchini, cut into slices

1 tablespoon olive oil

Salt and pepper, to taste

INSTRUCTIONS:

1. Make the Marinade: In a medium bowl, whisk together all of the marinade ingredients. Reserve half of the marinade and set aside. Add steak tips and marinate for at least 1 hour or as many as 24 hours.
2. Make the Steak and Vegetables: Preheat the oven to 400°F. Line a rimmed 13x18-inch sheet pan with parchment paper, or coat with nonstick cooking spray.
3. In a large bowl, toss red onion, bell pepper, asparagus, and zucchini with olive oil, salt, and pepper.
4. Place on the sheet pan in a single layer. Bake for 10–15 minutes.
5. Remove the sheet pan from the oven, and set the oven to broil.
6. Make room in the center of the sheet pan for the steak tips; lay them on the pan in a single layer.
7. Return the sheet pan to the oven for 5 minutes. Flip the sirloin tips over, and return to the oven for an additional 3 minutes, or until steak tips are to desired doneness.
8. Remove from the oven and allow to rest for 5 minutes. Serve with the reserved marinade.

Nutrition per serving: Calories: 434; Total Fat 32g; Net Carbs: 9g; Protein: 25g

Barbecue Pork Tenderloin with Green Beans and Tomatoes

PREP TIME: 15 minutes

TOTAL TIME: 40 minutes

COOK TIME: 25 minutes

YIELD: 6 servings

The seasoning below tastes good on all sorts of things, and is great in case you don't particularly like or have access to a sugar-free barbecue sauce. You could make a big batch and have it on hand for all your summer barbecue needs!

INGREDIENTS:

¼ cup paprika

3 tablespoons salt

3 tablespoons pepper

2 teaspoons garlic powder

2 teaspoons onion powder

1 teaspoon chipotle powder

1 teaspoon cumin

18-ounce pork tenderloin

1 pound green beans, trimmed

16 ounces cherry tomatoes, halved

2 tablespoons olive oil

Salt and pepper, to taste

INSTRUCTIONS:

1. Preheat oven to 425°F.
2. In a small bowl, whisk together dry ingredients.
3. Pat pork tenderloin dry with towel. Rub all over with the dry rub.
4. Spread green beans evenly over sheet pan. Top with cherry tomatoes. Drizzle with olive oil, salt, and pepper.
5. Place pork tenderloin on top of vegetables.
6. Bake in oven 25–30 minutes, or until internal temperature of pork reaches 145°F at thickest part.
7. Let tenderloin stand for 10 minutes before slicing.

Nutrition per serving: Calories: 177: Total Fat: 7g; Net Carbs: 8g; Protein: 18g

Parmesan Pork Chops with Asparagus

PREP TIME: 10 minutes
TOTAL TIME: 55 Minutes
COOK TIME: 45 minutes
YIELD: 4 servings

(Be careful with using Parmesan cheese from a canister; it often has added carbs that wouldn't be present if you use fresh. It's something to be aware of to be able to plan ahead for the day's macros.)

INGREDIENTS:

1 large jicama, cut into 1-inch chunks

3 tablespoons olive oil, divided

Salt and pepper, to taste

½ cup grated Parmesan cheese

½ cup crushed pork rinds

1 teaspoon garlic salt

½ teaspoon black pepper

4 boneless pork chops, ½ inch-thick

1 bunch asparagus, trimmed

INSTRUCTIONS:

1. Preheat the oven to 350°F. Line a rimmed 13x18-inch sheet pan with parchment paper or coat with nonstick cooking spray.
2. Place the jicama on the sheet pan in a single layer. Drizzle with 1 tablespoon olive oil and season with salt and pepper. Toss together so that they are evenly coated.
3. In a shallow dish, combine the Parmesan, pork rinds, garlic salt, and back pepper.
4. Place the pork chops on the sheet pan in a single layer. Drizzle with 1 tablespoon olive oil. Top with half of the Parmesan mixture.
5. Bake for 25 minutes.
6. Remove the sheet pan from the oven. Stir the jicama, then move to the side to make room for the asparagus.
7. Add the asparagus to the sheet pan. Drizzle with remaining olive oil. Top the jicama and asparagus with remaining Parmesan mixture.
8. Bake for an additional 20 minutes or until vegetables are cooked to desired tenderness.

Nutrition per serving: Calories: 392; Total Fat: 23g; Net Carbs: 7g; Protein: 37g

Keto tip: If you're trying to lose weight, remember that weight loss isn't linear, and the number on the scale can be misleading. Try tracking your measurements as well and see what a difference you get!

Beef Tenderloin with Brussels Sprouts

PREP TIME: 15 Minutes
TOTAL TIME: 65 Minutes
COOK TIME: 50 Minutes
YIELD: 4 servings

This makes for a lovely Sunday dinner—or supper, as some may call it. If you do not have fresh herbs, you can substitute dried herbs, but rub them between your hands to wake up the flavors before putting them in the sauce, and use about one third the quantity.

INGREDIENTS:

1½ pounds beef tenderloin

3 tablespoons olive oil, divided

Salt and pepper, to taste

1 pound Brussels sprouts, trimmed and halved

2 large shallots, chopped

1 tablespoon whole grain mustard

1 tablespoon red wine vinegar

1 tablespoon Worcestershire sauce

1 teaspoon fresh thyme, minced

1 teaspoon fresh rosemary, minced

1 teaspoon fresh oregano, minced

2 cloves garlic, minced

INSTRUCTIONS:

1. Preheat oven to 425°F. Line a rimmed 13x18-inch sheet pan with parchment paper, or coat with nonstick cooking spray.
2. Place tenderloin on the sheet pan; rub with 1 tablespoon olive oil and season with salt and pepper.
3. In a large bowl, toss Brussels sprouts and shallots with 1 tablespoon olive oil and season with salt and pepper. Arrange vegetables on the sheet pan in a single layer.
4. Bake for 12–15 minutes, or until vegetables are slightly tender.
5. Set the oven to broil. Broil, turning the beef every 2–3 minutes, until the vegetables are slightly charred, and the beef reaches an internal temperature of 128°F to 130°F for medium-rare.
6. Remove from oven and allow to rest at least 10 minutes.
7. In a small bowl, whisk together the mustard, red wine vinegar, Worcestershire sauce, herbs, garlic, and remaining olive oil. Pour slowly over beef and vegetables.

Nutrition per serving: Calories: 375; Total Fat: 26g; Net Carbs: 7g; Protein: 25g

Steak Fajitas

PREP TIME: 10 minutes
TOTAL TIME: 20 minutes
COOK TIME: 20 minutes
YIELD: 6–8 servings

(There are a lot of recipes out there now for keto tortillas. Give one a try! Or, serve this over a bed of lettuce or cauliflower rice. I like mine with lime and cilantro.)

INGREDIENTS:

2 garlic cloves, minced

1 teaspoon paprika

1 teaspoon cumin

½ teaspoon chili powder

2 tablespoons olive oil

¼ cup + 1 bunch cilantro, divided

2 tablespoons lime juice

2 pounds flank steak, sliced thin

1 yellow bell pepper

1 red bell pepper

2 jalapeño peppers, sliced

½ red onion, sliced

2 limes, sliced

1 bunch cilantro

INSTRUCTIONS:

1. Preheat oven to 425°F. Line a rimmed 13x18-inch sheet pan with parchment paper or coat with nonstick cooking spray.
2. In a large bowl, combine garlic, paprika, cumin, chili powder, olive oil, cilantro, and lime juice. Add steak, peppers, and onion; stir to combine. Set aside and allow to marinate for 10–15 minutes (or longer, if you're able).
3. Place lime slices in a single layer on the sheet pan
4. Place the steak and vegetables on the sheet pan, on top of the lime slices, spreading them out as evenly as possible. Bake for 10–15 minutes.
5. Set the oven to broil and leave sheet pan in oven for an additional 3 minutes.
6. Remove from oven and top with more cilantro.

Nutrition per serving: Calories: 307; Total Fat: 17g; Net Carbs: 5g; Protein: 33g

SEAFOOD & VEGETABLES

Thai-Glazed Salmon with Vegetables

PREP TIME: 5 minutes
TOTAL TIME: 30 minutes
COOK TIME: 25 minutes
YIELD: 4 servings

(Sweet and spicy come together in this delicious Thai-Glazed Salmon with veggies that will tantalize your taste buds!)

INGREDIENTS:

Thai Sweet Chili Sauce

1 red chili, chopped

½ tablespoon tomato paste

2 tablespoons sugar substitute

2 tablespoons rice vinegar

2 cloves garlic, crushed

½ teaspoon freshly grated ginger

½ teaspoon salt

4 salmon fillets

½ red bell pepper, chopped

½ green bell pepper, chopped

½ yellow bell pepper, chopped

1 onion, chopped

1 half cabbage, thinly sliced

½ cup Thai sweet chili sauce (recipe below)

¼ cup soy sauce or coconut aminos

1 tablespoon fresh grated ginger

1 tablespoon fresh lime juice

Pinch of red pepper flakes

Cilantro, chopped

1 lime, sliced thin

INSTRUCTIONS:

1. Make the Thai Sweet Chili Sauce: Place all ingredients for chili sauce into saucepan. Bring to a boil.
2. Reduce to a simmer, stirring frequently for 5 minutes.
3. Remove from heat and allow to cool.
4. Preheat oven to 475°F. Spray your sheet pan with cooking spray.
5. Lay the salmon skin-side down, surrounded by the chopped vegetables.
6. In a small bowl, whisk together Thai sweet chili sauce, soy sauce, ginger, lime juice, and red pepper flakes. Reserve ¼ cup of the marinade.
7. Pour the remaining marinade over the salmon and vegetables.
8. Cover with foil and bake for 15 minutes. Remove foil and change oven setting to broil.
9. Return pan to oven for another 5–7 minutes, until the top begins to turn black.
10. Remove pan from oven and brush remainder of marinade on top. Garnish with fresh cilantro and lime slices.

Nutrition per serving: Calories 139; Total Fat: 6g; Carbohydrates: 8g; Protein: 11g

Spanish Paella with Cauliflower "Rice"

PREP TIME: 5 minutes
TOTAL TIME: 20 minutes
COOK TIME: 15–18 minutes
YIELD: 6 servings

You can substitute Italian sweet sausage if you'd like to tone down the spice in this recipe. You can also use frozen cauliflower instead of fresh, but you will likely need to increase cooking time by 3–5 minutes. You will not need to thaw the cauliflower first.

INGREDIENTS:

2 tablespoons olive oil

3 cups fresh cauliflower, riced

½ cup red onion, chopped

½ cup bell pepper, chopped

3 garlic cloves, minced

2 bay leaves

1 lemon, zested

1 teaspoon paprika

1 pinch saffron

Crushed red pepper, to taste

Salt and pepper, to taste

1 cup chicken broth

1 pound large raw shrimp, cleaned

8 ounces spicy sausage

INSTRUCTIONS:

1. Preheat oven to 400°F.
2. Drizzle olive oil over sheet pan.
3. In a medium bowl, mix together cauliflower, onion, bell pepper, garlic, bay leaves, lemon zest, paprika, saffron, a pinch of crushed red pepper, salt, and pepper. Spread on sheet pan.
4. Pour chicken broth into sheet pan.
5. Roast in oven for 8 minutes, or until cauliflower is completely cooked. If the mixture is still wet, stir the mixture, leaving space on the sheet pan for moisture to evaporate.
6. Remove the sheet pan and add shrimp and sausage on top of veggies. Sprinkle with salt and pepper. Return to oven for 7–10 minutes.
7. Remove from oven and stir together.

Nutrition per serving: Calories: 262; Total Fat: 16g; Net Carbs: 6g; Protein: 20g

Pecan-Crusted Tilapia with Spinach and Tomatoes

PREP TIME: 10 minutes
TOTAL TIME: 28 minutes
COOK TIME: 18–20 minutes
YIELD: 4 servings

(Fish is a fantastic way to get your protein without too much fat. To choose good tilapia, look for flesh that has a bright white surface with no pink or brown spots. If buying frozen, it is best to buy fish that was frozen at sea.)

INGREDIENTS:

1½ cups pecans, crushed

½ teaspoon salt

½ teaspoon pepper

¼ teaspoon chili powder

2 eggs

4 tilapia fillets

1 package baby spinach

1 pint cherry tomatoes, halved

1 tablespoon olive oil

3 cloves garlic, sliced

2 lemons

Salt and pepper, to taste

INSTRUCTIONS:

1. Preheat oven to 350°F. Line a rimmed 13x18-inch sheet pan with parchment paper or coat with nonstick cooking spray.
2. In a shallow dish, combine the pecans, salt, pepper, and chili powder.
3. In another dish, beat the eggs with a fork.
4. Dip each tilapia fillet in the egg, then dip into the pecan mixture, making sure each fillet is completely covered.
5. Place each fillet on the sheet pan.
6. In a medium bowl, toss the spinach and tomatoes with olive oil, garlic, juice from 1 lemon, salt, and pepper. Place on sheet pan, next to fillets.
7. Bake for 15–18 minutes, or until the fish flakes easily with a fork.
8. Cut the second lemon into wedges and use for garnish.

Nutrition per serving: Calories: 390; Total Fat: 29g; Net carbs 3g; Protein: 31g

Chipotle-Lime Shrimp

PREP TIME: 10 minutes
TOTAL TIME: 50 minutes
COOK TIME: 40 minutes
YIELD: 4 servings

(I don't know why, but to me shrimp has always felt like a "fancy" food, which makes it perfect for parties. This meal will be sure to wow your friends, and will require very little effort from you!)

INGREDIENTS:

1 medium jicama, cubed

1 tablespoon olive oil

Salt and pepper, to taste

2 medium zucchini, chopped

⅓ cup lime juice

¼ cup unsalted butter, melted

1 teaspoon chipotle chili paste

2 cloves garlic, minced

1 teaspoon cumin

2 tablespoons minced fresh cilantro

2 pounds uncooked shrimp, peeled and deveined

3 limes, sliced

INSTRUCTIONS:

1. Preheat oven to 400°F. Line a rimmed 13x18-inch sheet pan with parchment paper, or coat with nonstick cooking spray.
2. Spread jicama on the sheet pan. Drizzle with olive oil and season with salt and pepper.
3. Bake the jicama for 35 minutes, stirring halfway through.
4. In a small bowl, combine lime juice, butter, chipotle chili paste, garlic, cumin, cilantro, and salt to taste.
5. Remove sheet pan from oven. Arrange zucchini, shrimp, and three sliced limes on top of jicama. Pour lime juice mixture over vegetables and shrimp.
6. Bake until shrimp turn pink and vegetables are tender, about 10 minutes.

Nutrition per serving: Calories: 259; Total Fat: 15g; Net Carbs: 9g; Protein: 15g

Parmesan-Crusted Salmon with Broccoli

PREP TIME: 5 minutes
TOTAL TIME: 25 minutes
COOK TIME: 20 minutes
YIELD: 4 servings

(I would highly recommend making a large portion of the garlic aioli mayonnaise and keeping it in the refrigerator. It is so good on almost any meat or veggie.)

INGREDIENTS:

2 cloves garlic

4 (6-ounce) skinless salmon fillets

¼ cup chopped parsley

3 tablespoons mayonnaise

3 teaspoons lemon juice

Sea salt, to taste

²/₃ cup grated Parmesan cheese

3 teaspoons lemon zest

½ teaspoon dried thyme

5 tablespoons + 2 teaspoons olive oil, divided

1½ pounds broccoli florets

INSTRUCTIONS:

1. Preheat oven to 425°F. Line a rimmed 13x18-inch sheet pan with parchment paper or coat with nonstick cooking spray.
2. First, roast the garlic. Cut off the top ½ inch of the head of garlic. Place on a large piece of aluminum foil and top with 2 teaspoons olive oil. Wrap completely in the aluminum foil. Place in oven for 20–25 minutes. Remove from oven and set aside.
3. In a small bowl, combine mayonnaise, garlic, lemon juice, and salt to taste. Brush onto each salmon fillet.
4. In another small bowl, combine Parmesan, lemon zest, thyme, and 3 tablespoons olive oil. Spread evenly on top of salmon fillets.
5. Toss broccoli with 2 tablespoons olive oil and sea salt. Spread on sheet pan in a single layer around salmon.
6. Bake for 12–15 minutes, until fillets have cooked through.

Nutrition per serving: Calories: 492; Total Fat: 30g; Net Carbs: 8g; Protein: 42g

Stuffed Portobello Mushrooms

PREP TIME: 10 minutes
TOTAL TIME: 18–22 minutes
COOK TIME: 8–12 minutes
YIELD: 4 servings

(I don't know what it is, but something about the flavor of the runny egg with the spinach is one of my favorite things ever. This dish works great for breakfast, lunch, or dinner.)

INGREDIENTS:

4 portobello mushroom caps, cleaned, stems removed

1 tablespoon olive oil

Salt and pepper, to taste

3 garlic cloves, minced

6 ounces baby spinach

Pinch red pepper flakes

1 cup cream cheese, softened

8 ounces grated Parmesan

4 large egg yolks

½ cup shredded mozzarella

INSTRUCTIONS:

1. Preheat oven to 450°F. Line a rimmed 13x18-inch sheet pan with parchment paper, or coat with nonstick cooking spray.
2. Brush mushroom caps lightly with olive oil and season with salt and pepper. Roast for 15 to 25 minutes, or until tender. Carefully discard any excess moisture that has collected.
3. In a medium sauté pan, heat olive oil over medium-high heat. Add garlic and stir until fragrant, about 1 minute. Add spinach and stir. Season with red pepper flakes, salt, and pepper. Stir until wilted. Remove from heat. Set aside.
4. In a medium bowl, combine cream cheese and about 1 teaspoon each of salt, pepper, and Parmesan.
5. Spoon equal amounts of spinach into each mushroom cap. Then spoon equal amounts of cream cheese mixture on top of spinach, leaving a well for the egg yolk.
6. Place an egg yolk into the well in each mushroom cap. Top with mozzarella cheese and some black pepper.
7. Bake for about 5 minutes or until cheese is melted and egg is just set.

Nutrition per serving: Calories: 383; Total Fat: 34g; Net Carbs: 5g; Protein: 15g

Tofu and Vegetables

PREP TIME: 10 minutes
TOTAL TIME: 45 minutes
COOK TIME: 35 minutes
YIELD: 4 servings

(Curry powder adds a powerful punch to this simple and very filling meal. As an alternative to curry powder, you can use equal amounts of coriander and cumin.)

INGREDIENTS:

16 ounces extra-firm tofu, cut into ½-inch cubes

¼ cup olive oil, divided

1 teaspoon curry powder

Salt and pepper, to taste

1 large bulb fennel, cored and cut into wedges

1 pint cherry tomatoes, halved

1 bunch asparagus, trimmed

INSTRUCTIONS:

1. Preheat oven to 400°F. Line a rimmed 13x18-inch sheet pan with parchment paper or coat with nonstick cooking spray.
2. Spread tofu cubes on a paper towel. Cover with a second paper towel and press to remove as much moisture as possible.
3. In a small bowl, combine 3 tablespoons olive oil, curry powder, salt, and pepper to taste. Add tofu and toss to coat.
4. Spread tofu on the sheet pan in a single layer. Add fennel, taking care not to overcrowd the pan. Roast 20 minutes.
5. Add tomatoes and asparagus to sheet pan. Drizzle with remaining olive oil and season with salt and pepper.
6. Roast an additional 15 minutes, until tomatoes are very soft and asparagus is al dente.

Nutrition per serving: Calories: 229; Total Fat: 24g; Net Carbs: 4g; Protein: 16g

Eggplant Parmesan

PREP TIME: 20 minutes
TOTAL TIME: 35 minutes
COOK TIME: 40 minutes
YIELD: 4 servings

Eggplant is a high-fiber, low-calorie food rich in nutrients that offers a multitude of health benefits. It can reduce the risk of heart disease, help with blood sugar levels, and assist in weight loss. It is also extremely versatile and easy to add to any diet.

INGREDIENTS:

2 eggs, beaten

¾ cup grated Parmesan cheese

2 tablespoons Italian seasoning

Salt and pepper, to taste

1 medium to large eggplant, sliced

2 tablespoons olive oil

1 jar low-sugar marinara sauce

½ pound fresh mozzarella, sliced

INSTRUCTIONS:

1. Preheat oven to 450°F. Line a rimmed 13x18-inch sheet pan with parchment paper or coat with nonstick cooking spray.
2. Heat the sheet pan in the oven for 10 minutes.
3. In a medium shallow dish, beat the eggs. Place the Parmesan, Italian seasoning, salt, and pepper in a second medium dish.
4. Dip each eggplant slice in egg, then into Parmesan mixture.
5. Remove sheet pan. Brush with olive oil.
6. Place the eggplant slices on the sheet pan in a single layer. Bake 8–10 minutes, or until undersides are crisp and browned. Flip slices over, and continue baking another 8–10 minutes, or until the other sides are also crisp and browned.
7. Remove the sheet pan from oven.
8. Top the eggplant with marinara sauce and mozzarella. Return the pan to the oven and bake another 20–25 minutes, until the cheese is melted. Rotate halfway through baking time.

Nutrition per serving: Calories: 414; Total Fat: 30g; Net Carbs: 5g; Protein: 29g

Zucchini Sausage Pizza Boats

PREP TIME: 15 minutes
TOTAL TIME: 40 minutes
COOK TIME: 20 minutes
YIELD: 4 servings

What is better than saucy, cheesy, pizza? Not much, as far as I'm concerned. These zucchini boats will hit that spot for sure. You can definitely swap out different toppings, if you prefer pepperoni or—God forbid—anchovies.

INGREDIENTS:

2 tablespoons olive oil

3 cloves garlic, minced

4–5 medium zucchinis, halved lengthwise and flesh scooped out

1 cup low-sugar marinara sauce

1 pound spicy Italian sausage, browned

1½ cups mozzarella cheese, shredded

Salt and pepper to taste

INSTRUCTIONS:

1. Preheat oven to 400°F. Line a rimmed 13x18-inch sheet pan with parchment paper or coat with nonstick cooking spray.
2. In a small saucepan, warm olive oil and garlic over medium heat until garlic is just browned. Remove from heat.
3. Place zucchini boats on sheet pan. Brush each with a generous amount of garlic-infused olive oil. Top with equal amounts of marinara sauce, then sausage. Top with equal amounts of mozzarella cheese.
4. Bake for 18–20 minutes, or until cheese is melted and golden brown. Add salt and pepper as desired.

Nutrition per serving: Calories: 420; Total Fat: 28g; Net Carbs: 9g; Protein: 34g

Cauliflower Nachos

PREP TIME: 15 minutes
TOTAL TIME: 35 minutes
COOK TIME: 20 minutes
YIELD: 8 servings

(There aren't many great keto replacements for nachos. I think you may be convinced with these, though. To make prep even easier, you can use a rotisserie chicken.)

INGREDIENTS:

1 head cauliflower, cut into florets

2 tablespoons olive oil

3 cloves garlic, minced

1 teaspoon cumin

½ teaspoon chili powder

½ teaspoon paprika

Salt and pepper, to taste

1 pound chicken, cooked, diced

1 cup shredded cheddar cheese

1 tomato, diced

⅓ cup guacamole

½ medium red onion, diced

1–2 jalapeños, sliced

2 tablespoons fresh cilantro, chopped

INSTRUCTIONS:

1. Preheat oven to 425°F. Line a rimmed 13x18-inch sheet pan with parchment paper, or coat with nonstick cooking spray.
2. In a large bowl or on the sheet pan, toss cauliflower florets with olive oil, garlic, cumin, chili powder, and paprika. Season with salt and pepper, to taste.
3. Bake for 12–14 minutes, until fork-tender. Remove from oven.
4. Top with chicken and cheese. Return to oven and bake 5–6 more minutes, or until cheese is melted.
5. Serve topped with tomato, guacamole, red onion, jalapeños, and cilantro.

Nutrition per serving: Calories: 358; Total Fat: 22g; Net Carbs: 8g; Protein: 8g

Asian Salmon with Bok Choy

PREP TIME: 20 minutes
TOTAL TIME: 40–45 minutes
COOK TIME: 20–25 minutes
YIELD: 4 servings

Salmon is rich in omega-3 fatty acids, which have a lot of heart-related benefits. It is also a great source of lean protein and potassium. Many would argue that it is one of the world's healthiest foods. In fact, the American Heart Association recommends eating at least two 3½-ounce servings of fatty fish like salmon every week.

INGREDIENTS:

⅓ cup soy sauce or coconut aminos

2 tablespoons rice vinegar

2 tablespoons sweetener

1 tablespoon + 2 teaspoon sesame oil, divided

½ teaspoon garlic salt

4 skinless salmon fillets

1½ pounds baby bok choy, halved, bottom removed

Salt and pepper, to taste

INSTRUCTIONS:

1. Preheat oven to 400°F. Line a rimmed 13x18-inch sheet pan with parchment paper or coat with nonstick cooking spray.
2. In a small bowl, whisk together the soy sauce, vinegar, sweetener, 1 tablespoon sesame oil, and garlic salt.
3. Place the salmon on the sheet pan. Brush on both sides with the glaze.
4. Add bok choy to sheet pan in a single layer. Drizzle with remaining sesame oil and salt and pepper.
5. Bake for 10–12 minutes, or until the salmon flakes easily.

Nutrition per serving: Calories: 180; Total Fat: 5g; Net Carbs: 4g; Protein: 27g

Garlic Butter Shrimp

PREP TIME: 15 minutes
TOTAL TIME: 25 minutes
COOK TIME: 10 minutes
YIELD: 4 servings

(This dish is best paired with a light salad or cauliflower rice to contrast with the heaviness of the butter.)

INGREDIENTS:

½ cup butter, melted

4 cloves garlic, minced

1 tablespoon lemon juice

½ teaspoon dried Italian seasoning

Salt and pepper, to taste

2 lemons, sliced

1½ pounds medium shrimp, peeled and deveined

2 tablespoons chopped fresh parsley

INSTRUCTIONS:

1. Preheat oven to 400°F. Line a rimmed 13x18-inch sheet pan with parchment paper or coat with nonstick cooking spray.
2. In a small bowl, combine butter, garlic, lemon juice, Italian seasoning, salt, and pepper, to taste.
3. Lay slices of lemon in a single layer on the sheet pan.
4. Place shrimp on the sheet pan in a single layer on top of the lemon slices. Drizzle butter mixture over the shrimp and gently toss to combine.
5. Bake for 8–10 minutes or until shrimp is pink, firm, and cooked through.

Nutrition per serving: Calories: 386; Total Fat: 26g; Net Carbs: 3g; Protein: 37g

Fish in Brown Butter Sauce

PREP TIME: 15 minutes
TOTAL TIME: 45 minutes
COOK TIME: 30 minutes
YIELD: 4 servings

Radishes are a super versatile food for those avoiding carbs; I have known people to use sliced radishes as a "chip" to dip into things. They also make an amazing substitute for potatoes. Not only that, they offer several health benefits; they are good source of fiber, so they will help keep you regular. They are also a good source of Vitamin C, which helps battle free radicals in your body to prevent cell damage and keep you looking and feeling young!

INGREDIENTS:

1 pound radishes, halved
2 tablespoons olive oil, divided
Salt and pepper, to taste
4 (6-ounce) haddock fillets
1 pound green beans, trimmed
8 tablespoons butter
1 lemon, zested and juiced
3 tablespoons Dijon mustard

Keto tip: Can you drink alcohol on keto? Yes! Most plain liquors are 0 carbs (NOT 0 calories, though): vodka, tequila, rum, gin, whiskey. However, once you are keto, alcohol may affect you differently, so go slowly. Otherwise you may be nursing a massive hangover the next day.

INSTRUCTIONS:

1. Preheat the oven to 400°F. Line a rimmed 13x18-inch sheet pan with parchment paper or coat with nonstick cooking spray.
2. Toss radishes with 1 tablespoon olive oil, and add salt and pepper to taste. Bake for 10 minutes.
3. Remove sheet pan from oven. Add haddock and green beans so that everything is in a single layer. Drizzle fish and green beans with remaining olive oil and season with salt and pepper.
4. Return to the oven and bake for an additional 10–15 minutes or until fish flakes easily with a fork.
5. In a small saucepan, melt the butter, stirring occasionally. Once melted, cook until the butter starts to brown on the bottom and it begins to smell slightly nutty. Remove from heat and immediately pour into a small bowl.
6. In the same small bowl, whisk butter together with lemon zest, lemon juice, and mustard.
7. Either pour sauce over fish once plated, or serve on the side for dipping.

Nutrition per serving: Calories: 520; Total Fat: 32g; Net Carbs: 8g; Protein: 44g

Cauliflower "Fried" Rice

PREP TIME: 15 minutes
TOTAL TIME: 40 minutes
COOK TIME: 25 minutes
YIELD: 4 servings

This tastes like Chinese takeout, but is so much better for you! You can use ground ginger instead of fresh, but I think the fresh makes a *huge* difference in flavor. You could also easily swap out the protein in this to steak, pork, or shrimp.

INGREDIENTS:

1 teaspoon salt

½ teaspoon freshly grated ginger

½ teaspoon black pepper

Pinch red pepper flakes

3 cups cauliflower, riced, or frozen cauliflower

1 small onion, minced

7–8 broccoli florets, diced

3 garlic cloves, minced

3 tablespoons butter, melted

3 tablespoons soy sauce or coconut aminos, divided

1 tablespoon sesame oil

4 eggs, scrambled

½ pound chicken breast, cooked, diced

2 scallions, sliced thin

Salt and pepper, to taste

INSTRUCTIONS:

1. Preheat oven to 400°F. Line a rimmed 13x18-inch sheet pan with parchment paper, or coat with nonstick cooking spray.
2. In a small bowl, combine the salt, ginger, pepper, and red pepper flakes.
3. Toss together the cauliflower, onion, and broccoli with butter and spices. Spread on the sheet pan into a single layer.
4. Drizzle 2 tablespoons soy sauce or coconut aminos over the entire mixture.
5. Roast for 25–30 minutes or until it starts to become golden brown/toasted.
6. Remove from oven and gently toss together. Add the remaining soy sauce, sesame oil, eggs, and chicken, tossing until combined.
7. Top with scallions. Add salt and pepper as desired.

Nutrition per serving: Calories: 309; Total Fat: 18g; Net Carbs: 6g; Protein: 26g

Spicy Cauliflower and Ham "Mac" and Cheese

PREP TIME: 15 minutes
TOTAL TIME: 40 minutes
COOK TIME: 25 minutes
YIELD: 4 servings

(You can vary the spiciness of this recipe by leaving the seeds in the jalapeño, and/or adding an additional jalapeño. Cooking the cauliflower just until crisp-tender is equivalent to cooking pasta to just shy of "al dente" so that it doesn't overcook and become mushy in the oven.)

INGREDIENTS:

1 large head fresh cauliflower, cut into small florets

¼ cup butter

½ cup heavy cream

½ cup chicken broth

½ teaspoon dry mustard

¼ teaspoon nutmeg

8 ounces sharp cheddar cheese, shredded

2 ounces cream cheese

1 jalapeño, diced

10 ounces ham, cubed

6 ounces sharp cheddar cheese, sliced

2 tablespoons butter, sliced

Salt and pepper, to taste

INSTRUCTIONS:

1. Preheat oven to 375°F. Line a rimmed 13x18-inch sheet pan with parchment paper or coat with nonstick cooking spray.
2. Bring a large pot of salted water to a boil. Add cauliflower, and boil just until crisp-tender. Drain well and rinse with cold water. Pat dry with paper towel. Set aside.
3. In a medium saucepan, melt butter. Add heavy cream and chicken broth, and whisk until heated through. Add dry mustard and nutmeg. Slowly add in 8 ounces of the shredded cheese a handful at a time, allowing to melt each time. Add the cream cheese and jalapeño, and whisk until cream cheese is melted.
4. In a large bowl, toss cauliflower with cheese sauce and ham. Pour onto sheet pan and spread into a single layer.
5. Top with alternating slices of cheddar cheese and butter. Sprinkle with salt and pepper, if desired.
6. Bake for 15–20 minutes, or until cheese on top is melted and browned.

Nutrition per serving: Calories: 386; Total Fat: 33g; Net Carbs: 6g; Protein: 16g

Spicy Shrimp with Baby Bok Choy

PREP TIME: 10 minutes

TOTAL TIME: 22–25 minutes

COOK TIME: 12–15 minutes

YIELD: 4 servings

(If you find yourself craving something sweet, it can be helpful to "distract" your taste buds with something fatty or salty—or even spicy. Feeding the craving is usually counterproductive. Try pickles, or some almond butter, or some of this shrimp!)

INGREDIENTS:

1½ pounds baby bok choy, cut in half lengthwise

3 tablespoons olive oil, divided

1½ teaspoons salt, divided

½ teaspoon red pepper flakes

1 tablespoon soy sauce or coconut aminos

1½ pounds shrimp, peeled and deveined

1 scallion, sliced thin

1 lemon, cut into 4 wedges

INSTRUCTIONS:

1. Preheat oven to 450°F. Line a rimmed 13x18-inch sheet pan with parchment paper, or coat with nonstick cooking spray.
2. In a medium bowl, combine bok choy with 2 tablespoons olive oil and ½ teaspoon salt. Arrange in a single layer on the sheet pan, leaving room for the shrimp.
3. Put sheet pan with bok choy into the oven for 5 minutes.
4. In the same medium bowl, combine remaining oil, red pepper flakes, soy sauce, and ½ teaspoon salt. Add shrimp and toss to combine.
5. Remove sheet pan from oven after 5 minutes; add shrimp and return to oven for an additional 8 to 10 minutes, until shrimp is pink.
6. Serve with scallions and lemon wedges.

Nutrition per serving: Calories: 235; Total Fat: 14g; Net Carbs: 1g; Protein: 44g

Sweet Citrus Salmon

PREP TIME: 10 Minutes

TOTAL TIME: 20 Minutes

COOK TIME: 8–10 minutes

YIELD: 4 servings

(Lemons have tons of health benefits, one of which is improved blood flow to the brain. They also have more than 20 anticancer compounds, and are also known as a cleansing agent both for your digestive system and also to purify your blood.)

Keto tip: It is very important to make sure you get enough salt into your diet, but oversalting your food is not going to be enough. I have found that large, coarse salt is the easiest way to do it—just doing a handful of it like a shot. The other option is to buy empty supplement capsules and fill them with salt. For more details about how much salt to take in each day, see the links in the introduction.

INGREDIENTS:

Citrus Glaze:

Juice of 1 lime

Juice of 1 lemon

1 tablespoon orange extract

Zest of 1 orange

1 teaspoon freshly grated ginger

1 tablespoon butter

Pinch xantham gum

1 tablespoons soy sauce or coconut aminos

1 tablespoon sweetener or brown sugar substitute

1 tablespoon sriracha

3 cloves garlic, minced

Salmon and Vegetables:

1 pound asparagus, trimmed

1 tablespoon olive oil

Salt and pepper, to taste

4 (6-ounce) salmon fillets

INSTRUCTIONS:

1. Preheat oven to 400°F. Line a rimmed 13x18-inch sheet pan with parchment paper, or coat with nonstick cooking spray.
2. In a saucepan, whisk together the juices, extract, zest, and ginger over medium heat and bring to a simmer. Continue whisking at a simmer until the juices thicken, about 10 minutes. Add the butter and whisk until it melts. Add a pinch of xantham gum and stir constantly until the glaze reaches the desired thickness.
3. In a medium bowl or on the sheet pan, combine the asparagus with the olive oil, salt, and pepper. Lay in a single layer.
4. Lay the salmon fillets on the sheet pan. Pat dry with paper towels, and sprinkle with salt. Pour half of the glaze over the salmon fillets.
5. Bake for 10–12 minutes, or until salmon reaches an internal temperature of 145°F and flakes easily with a fork.
6. Brush the salmon with the remaining glaze.

Nutrition per serving: Calories: 367; Total Fat: 22g; Net Carbs: 8g; Protein: 31g

DESSERTS

Chocolate Mousse Bars

PREP TIME: 20 minutes
YIELD: 16 servings

(Chocolate cream pie on a graham cracker crust has always been a favorite of mine, especially at the holidays. Being able to make a keto version is awesome! If you don't have powdered sweetener, you can put granulated sweetener in the blender until it becomes a fine powder.)

INGREDIENTS:

Crust:

1 cup ground pecans

2 cups almond flour

$^2/_3$ cup powdered erythritol

2 teaspoons cinnamon

½ cup butter, melted

Mousse:

1 cup heavy whipping cream

1 small box sugar-free chocolate instant pudding

Pudding:

2 cups unsweetened almond milk (I used the chocolate unsweetened)

1 large box sugar-free chocolate instant pudding

INSTRUCTIONS:

1. Line a 9x13-inch rimmed sheet pan with parchment paper.
2. In a medium bowl, combine the ingredients for the crust. Press into the bottom of the sheet pan.
3. In a medium bowl, beat the mousse ingredients on high until the mixture is firm.
4. Spread on top of crust.
5. In a large bowl, combine the pudding ingredients. Spread on top of mousse.
6. Refrigerate for at least 2 hours.

Nutrition per serving: Calories: 193; Total Fat: 18g; Net Carbs: 7g; Protein: 2

Cheesecake Bars with Blackberry Sauce

PREP TIME: 15 minutes
TOTAL TIME: 1 hour, 15 minutes
COOK TIME: 60 minutes
YIELD: 20 servings

I love blackberry flavor in any capacity, so it made sense to me to make this a blackberry sauce. However, if you do not have the same passion for blackberries that I do, you can make a mixed berry sauce or any other berry sauce. Just use the same volume of other berries, and voilà!

INGREDIENTS:

Crust:
2 cups almond flour
⅓ cup powdered erythritol
⅓ cup unsweetened cocoa
½ cup butter, melted

Cheesecake Filling:
40 ounces cream cheese, softened
1½ cups powdered sweetener

3 eggs, room temperature
1 tablespoon orange extract
Zest of 1 orange
1 teaspoon vanilla

Blackberry Sauce:
18 ounces blackberries
¼ cup sweetener
1 teaspoon xantham gum (more or less, depending on desired thickness)

INSTRUCTIONS:

1. Preheat oven to 350°F. Line a rimmed 9x13-inch sheet pan with parchment paper or coat with nonstick cooking spray.
2. Make the Crust: In a medium bowl, combine the ingredients for the crust. Press into the bottom of the sheet pan.
3. Make the Filling: In a large bowl, beat the cream cheese and powdered sweetener together on medium speed, until the mixture is fluffy. Beat in the eggs one at a time. (Pro tip: Crack the eggs into a bowl before putting them into the cream cheese mixture. It's easier to avoid getting shells in your mix!) Beat in the orange extract, orange zest, and vanilla.
4. Pour the filling on top of the crust, smoothing with a spatula.
5. Bake for 45–55 minutes, until the center is almost set.
6. Make the Blackberry Sauce: In a small saucepan, whisk together the blackberries and sweetener on medium heat. Continue to whisk together for 15 minutes; add xantham gum. Whisk for an additional 5 minutes, until desired thickness is reached.
7. Serve cheesecake bars with blackberry sauce.

Nutrition per serving: Calories: 238; Total Fat: 21g; Net Carbs: 7g; Protein: 5g

Margarita Bars

PREP TIME: 20 minutes
TOTAL TIME: 55 minutes
COOK TIME: 35 minutes
YIELD: 16 servings

(I'm not gonna lie: I enjoy a drink now and then. As a mom, it sometimes becomes vital to my family's survival. Tequila is definitely my favorite, and I have missed margaritas. These bars are the perfect summertime boozy treat. Feel free to leave out the tequila and sub in some additional lime juice if you prefer.)

INGREDIENTS:

Crust:

2 cups almond flour

⅓ cup powdered erythritol

2 tablespoons orange zest

2 tablespoons coarse salt

½ cup butter, melted

Filling:

5 eggs

2½ cups sweetener

½ cup lime juice

1½ teaspoons lime zest

1 teaspoon orange extract

1½ tablespoons tequila

Pinch of xantham gum

INSTRUCTIONS:

1. Preheat the oven to 350°F. Line a rimmed 9x13-inch sheet pan with parchment paper or coat with nonstick cooking spray.
2. Make the Crust: In a medium bowl, combine the ingredients for the crust. Press into the bottom of the sheet pan. Bake for 10 minutes, or until it begins to turn golden brown.
3. Make the Filling: In a medium bowl, whisk together the eggs and sweetener. Add juice, lime zest, orange extract, and tequila, and whisk until combined. Whisk in xantham gum.
4. Slowly pour filling over baked crust. Bake for 20–25 minutes or until top is set and starts to turn brown.
5. Allow to cool completely before serving.

Nutrition per serving: Calories: 108; Total Fat: 9g; Net Carbs: 7g; Protein: 3g

Texas Sheet Cake

PREP TIME: 15 minutes
TOTAL TIME: 45 minutes
COOK TIME: 30 minutes
YIELD: 16

No worries if you don't like coffee—the coffee does not actually show up as a flavor in this cake. If you don't have coffee at home, there are plenty of small bottles of black iced coffee available at your grocery store or gas station!

INGREDIENTS:

Cake:

1¼ cups almond flour

⅓ cup coconut flour

½ cup sweetener

3 tablespoons cocoa powder

2 teaspoons baking powder

¼ teaspoon salt

⅓ cup butter, melted

⅓ cup strong brewed coffee, cooled

3 tablespoons heavy cream

2 large eggs

¼ teaspoon almond extract

½ teaspoon vanilla

Frosting:

⅓ cup butter

3 tablespoons cocoa powder

3 tablespoons heavy cream

3 tablespoons water

½ teaspoon vanilla

1 cup powdered sweetener

Pinch xantham gum

½ cup pecans, chopped

INSTRUCTIONS:

1. Preheat oven to 325°F. Line a rimmed 9x13-inch sheet pan with parchment paper or coat with nonstick cooking spray.
2. Make the Cake: In a medium bowl, stir together the flours, sweetener, cocoa, baking powder, and salt.
3. In a large bowl, combine butter, coffee, and heavy cream. Mix in the eggs, one at a time. (Pro tip: Crack the eggs into a bowl first to avoid getting shells in the batter.) Add almond and vanilla extracts, and stir until combined.
4. Slowly add the dry ingredients into the wet, about ⅓ at a time.
5. Pour into sheet pan. Bake 15–20 minutes, until cake is set and toothpick inserted into center comes out clean.
6. Make the Frosting: In a medium saucepan, combine butter, cocoa powder, cream, and water. Whisk together until combined. Bring to a simmer, whisking the whole time. Add vanilla.
7. Stir in powdered sweetener, about ¼ cup at a time, continuing to whisk. Once completely incorporated, add xantham gum.
8. While the frosting is still hot, pour it over the cake, and sprinkle with pecans. Allow to cool until frosting is set. It is best to keep this cake in the fridge so it will remain firm.

Nutrition per serving: Calories: 210; Total Fat: 17g; Net Carbs: 2g; Protein: 4g

Raspberry Brownies

PREP TIME: 15 minutes
TOTAL TIME: 30 minutes
COOK TIME: 15 minutes
YIELD: 20 servings

(These brownies are so fudgy and delicious and so low in carbs, they will satisfy even the most intense chocolate craving.)

INGREDIENTS:

¾ cup almond flour

1¾ cups powdered sweetener, divided

½ cup cocoa

¾ teaspoon baking powder

1 cup (2 sticks) butter

6 ounces dark chocolate, chopped, divided

3 eggs, room temperature

1 teaspoon vanilla

1 container (6 ounces) raspberries

½ teaspoon lemon juice

¼ teaspoon xanthum gum

INSTRUCTIONS:

1. Preheat oven 325°F. Line a rimmed 9x13-inch sheet pan with parchment paper or coat with butter.
2. In a medium bowl, mix together almond flour, 1½ cups sweetener, cocoa, and baking powder.
3. In a large microwave-safe bowl, melt the butter and 4 ounces chocolate for 30 seconds–1 minute, or until fully melted. Mix in the eggs one at a time, stirring after each addition. Add vanilla and stir just to combine. Mix in the dry ingredients, just until combined, being careful not to overmix.
4. Add in remaining chopped chocolate, stirring just to combine.
5. Pour into lined sheet pan and smooth over the top.
6. In a small saucepan, heat the raspberries, lemon juice, and 2 tablespoons sweetener on low heat until raspberries break down and combine with the sweetener, and sauce is heated through. Strain to remove seeds. Set aside.
7. Return raspberries and pan to stove top on medium heat and add xantham gum, whisking constantly until thickens (1–2 minutes). Remove from heat and set aside.
8. Add raspberry sauce to top of brownies, and swirl throughout with a knife.
9. Bake for 26–32 minutes, until the center is set and a toothpick inserted into the center comes out moist.
10. Refrigerate for 30 minutes–2 hours.

Nutrition per serving: Calories: 129; Total Fat: 13g; Net Carbs: 3g; Protein: 2g

No-Bake Chocolate Peanut Butter Bars

PREP TIME: 10 minutes
YIELD: 24

One of my family's dominating holiday traditions are what we call "bonbons"; they are these peanut butter balls with crisp rice cereal inside and coated with chocolate. It doesn't ever really feel like Christmas until we have these, and now I have a replacement! These are so easy to make, and ridiculously delicious.

INGREDIENTS:

2½ cups almond flour

6½ ounces butter, melted

¾ cup powdered sweetener

1²/₃ cup nut butter

2 teaspoons vanilla

1¾ cup sugar-free chocolate chips, melted

INSTRUCTIONS:

1. Prepare a rimmed 9x13-inch sheet pan with parchment paper, or coat with nonstick cooking spray.
2. In a medium bowl, combine almond flour, butter, powdered sweetener, nut butter, and vanilla. Spread into the prepared baking sheet.
3. Spread the melted chocolate on top of the bars.
4. Refrigerate for a minimum of 1 hour or until chocolate hardens.

Nutrition info: Calories: 246; Total Fat: 21g; Net Carbs: 2g; Protein: 6g

No-Bake "Granola" Bars

PREP TIME: 10 minutes
YIELD: 24 servings

(If you have kids, you know that granola bars are a great, go-to snack. However, you also know that the ones you buy at the store are full of not-great things, like sugar. These are the kind of granola bars you can feel good about you or your kids eating.)

INGREDIENTS:

¾ cup flaxseed

1 cup unsweetened coconut flakes

3 tablespoons hemp hearts/seeds

¾ cup pecans, chopped

¾ cup walnuts, chopped

¾ cup almonds, chopped

¾ teaspoon salt

¾ cup nut butter (I used almond)

⅓ cup butter, melted

¼ cup powdered sweetener

¾ teaspoon vanilla

1 tablespoon cinnamon

INSTRUCTIONS:

1. Prepare a rimmed 9x13-inch sheet pan with parchment paper, or coat with nonstick cooking spray.
2. Combine the flaxseed, coconut flakes, hemp hearts, pecans, walnuts, almonds, and salt in a food processor or blender. Process on high until the mixture resembles coarse sand.
3. In a large bowl, mix the nut butter and melted butter together until smooth. Add the sweetener, vanilla, and cinnamon. Add the flaxseed and coconut mixture and stir until well combined.
4. Transfer to the sheet pan and spread evenly into pan.
5. Refrigerate at least one hour, then cut into bars.

Nutrition per serving: Calories: 185; Total Fat: 21g; Net Carbs: 2g; Protein: 3g

Peanut Butter and Jelly Sheet Cake

PREP TIME: 15 minutes
TOTAL TIME: 35 minutes
COOK TIME: 20 minutes
YIELD: 18 servings

This cake is a super fun way to enjoy a classic from everyone's childhood! You can substitute any nut butter for the peanut butter if you are following strict keto, which does not allow for peanuts.

INGREDIENTS:

1½ cups almond flour

¼ cup coconut flour

3 teaspoons baking powder

½ teaspoon salt

⅓ cup heavy cream

2 teaspoons vinegar

⅓ cup butter, melted

½ cup peanut butter

½ cup granulated sweetener

2 large eggs

¾ teaspoon vanilla

Strawberry Glaze:

2 pounds strawberries, washed, hulled, and diced

½ cup powdered sweetener

2 tablespoons lemon juice

Pinch of xantham gum

INSTRUCTIONS:

1. Preheat oven to 350°F. Line a rimmed 9x13-inch sheet pan with parchment paper, or coat with nonstick cooking spray.
2. Make the Cake: In a medium bowl, whisk together almond flour, coconut flour, baking powder, and salt.
3. In a small bowl, combine heavy cream and vinegar. Set aside.
4. In a large bowl, combine butter and peanut butter until smooth. Beat in sweetener. Add eggs one at a time, then add vanilla.
5. Add in ⅓ of the flour mixture and beat until combined; beat in heavy cream and vinegar mixture. Add in remaining flour mixture in 2 batches.
6. Pour batter into sheet pan. Bake for 18–22 minutes or until toothpick inserted in center comes out clean. Remove from oven and allow to cool.
7. Make the Glaze: In a medium saucepan, add the strawberries, sweetener, and lemon juice. Heat over medium-low heat for approximately 10 minutes, stirring constantly, until strawberries break down.
8. Add pinch of xantham gum and stir until thickened, an additional 2–3 minutes.
9. Allow glaze to cool; spread over top of cake.

Nutrition per serving: Calories: 176; Total Fat: 14g; Net Carbs: 3g; Protein: 5

Blueberry Zucchini Bars

PREP TIME: 30 minutes
TOTAL TIME: 1 hour
COOK TIME: 30 minutes
YIELD: 16 servings

(I love summertime, and these bars are the perfect marriage between two foods that are abundant in the summertime—zucchini and blueberries.)

INGREDIENTS:

⅓ cup heavy cream

1 teaspoon vinegar

2 cups zucchini, shredded

2 teaspoons lemon zest

1 tablespoon lemon juice

¾ cup butter, softened

1½ cups granulated sweetener

3 large eggs

1½ teaspoons vanilla

2¾ cups almond flour

2¾ teaspoons baking powder

½ teaspoon salt

1¼ cups blueberries (fresh or frozen)

INSTRUCTIONS:

1. Preheat the oven to 350°F. Line a 9x13-inch sheet pan with parchment paper, or coat with nonstick cooking spray.
2. In a small bowl, combine the heavy cream and vinegar. Set aside and let rest for 5 minutes.
3. In a medium bowl, combine zucchini, heavy cream mixture, lemon zest, and lemon juice, stirring until mixed thoroughly.
4. In a large bowl, beat together butter and sweetener until fluffy. Beat in eggs, one at a time. Add vanilla and stir to combine.
5. In another large bowl, whisk together almond flour, baking powder, and salt. Add a small portion to the butter and sweetener mixture, then add a small portion of the zucchini mixture, mixing well with each new addition. Continue this until all are completely combined. Fold in blueberries.
6. Pour batter into prepared pan. Bake for 30–35 minutes or until light golden brown and a toothpick inserted in the center comes out clean.

Nutrition per serving: Calories: 190; Total Fat: 18g; Net Carbs: 2; Protein: 4g

Lemon Bars

PREP TIME: 15 minutes
TOTAL TIME: 1 hour
COOK TIME: 45 minutes
YIELD: 14 servings

(I really enjoy lemon bars; I very clearly remember eating them in the hospital when I had my first child, so I have an emotional attachment to them. These are wonderfully light and tart—exactly the lemony goodness you're looking for!)

INGREDIENTS:

Crust:

3 cups almond flour

⅓ cup powdered sweetener

¼ cup fresh ginger, grated

¾ teaspoon ground ginger

½ teaspoon lemon zest

½ cup butter, melted

Filling:

6 tablespoons lemon juice

Zest of 1 lemon

3 large eggs

1⅓ cups powdered sweetener

⅓ cup almond flour

½ teaspoon baking powder

INSTRUCTIONS:

1. Preheat oven to 350°F. Line a rimmed 9x13-inch sheet pan with parchment paper or coat with nonstick cooking spray.
2. Make the Crust: In a medium bowl, combine almond flour, sweetener, fresh ginger, ground ginger, and lemon zest. Pour in the butter and mix together.
3. Press into prepared sheet pan. Bake for 10 minutes, then set aside.
4. Make the Filling: In a large bowl, beat all of the filling ingredients together until well blended.
5. Pour the filling onto the baked crust.
6. Bake for 15–20 minutes or until the top is golden brown.

Nutrition per serving: Calories: 175; Total Fat: 10g; Net Carbs: 4g; Protein: 3g

Cookie Dough Cheesecake

PREP TIME: 30 Minutes
YIELD: 20 servings

(Try not to eat the entire thing once it sets, I dare you.
No, seriously, don't do it. It wouldn't be good for you.)

INGREDIENTS:

Cookie Dough:

2¾ cups almond flour

3 teaspoons coconut flour

½ cup butter, softened

3 ounces cream cheese, softened

¾ cup sweetener

¾ cup sugar-free chocolate chips

Cheesecake:

1 cup heavy whipping cream

24 ounces cream cheese, softened

1 cup powdered sweetener

1 teaspoon vanilla

INSTRUCTIONS:

1. Prepare a rimmed 9x13-inch sheet pan with parchment paper or coat with nonstick cooking spray.
2. Make the Cookie Dough: Stir together the flours, butter, cream cheese, and sweetener until smooth. Add the chocolate chips and stir.
3. Make the Cheesecake: Beat the whipping cream until soft peaks form. Set aside in the refrigerator.
4. Beat the cream cheese, sweetener, and vanilla until creamy. Add the whipped cream and beat until combined.
5. Spread the cheesecake on top of the base evenly.
6. Refrigerate for a minimum of 4 hours.

Nutrition per serving: Calories: 269; Total Fat: 25g; Net Carbs: 3g; Protein: 5g

Dark Chocolate Almond Coconut Bark

PREP TIME: 15 minutes
YIELD: 24 servings

(This is an excellent low-calorie treat or snack for any time of day.)

INGREDIENTS:

1 cup almonds

1 cup unsweetened coconut flakes

1–2 tablespoon coconut oil, melted

1 teaspoon cinnamon

3 tablespoon granulated sweetener

6 ounces 90% dark chocolate or sugar-free chocolate

1 cup coconut butter

Coarse sea salt

INSTRUCTIONS:

1. Preheat oven to 350°F. Line a rimmed sheet pan (any size) with parchment paper.
2. In a medium bowl, combine almonds, coconut flakes, coconut oil, cinnamon, and sweetener. Spread the almonds and coconut on the sheet pan in a single layer.
3. Bake for 5–8 minutes, keeping a close eye on it to avoid burning. Remove from oven, pour into a bowl, and set aside.
4. Add a new sheet of parchment paper to your sheet pan.
5. In a double boiler, melt the chocolate. Once it has begun to melt, add the coconut butter.
6. Once completely melted, pour onto the lined sheet pan. Top with almonds, coconut, and sea salt. Pat down lightly with your hands to ensure that everything is touching the chocolate.
7. Allow to cool in the refrigerator for a minimum of 1 hour. Break apart as desired.

Nutrition per serving: Calories: 110; Total Fat: 11g; Net Carbs: 0g; Protein: 1g

Acknowledgments

I have wanted to write a book since I was very young. I also discovered a love of cooking at a fairly young age, performing cooking shows in my kitchen by myself. Somehow, those two passions and dreams combined in the opportunity to write this cookbook. For that, I would like to thank my friend and editor, Abigail Gehring, who in so many ways has supported and loved me in the four years we have known each other. I could never have expected we would become such good friends, but I'm so glad you are in my life, and am so thankful you gave me this chance.

There are so many people who have stood by me throughout my life, and without that longtime support, I don't think I would have been able to accomplish this book with all of the other things going on in my daily life. Jessica Willis, Katy Emond, Amanda Whitney Daniels, Amy Boemig, Bethany Carpenter, Tim Lawrence, Melanie French, Barbara French, Jason Madden, Dawn Grobe, Allysen Fitzpatrick, Heidi White, Melissa Burbank, Rozanna Waller, I thank you all so much for everything you have done, and I hope I have done—or one day can do—the same for you.

I have the best family in the world, especially the women who have always shown me how incredibly strong women can be. Also to my dad, who has always been so supportive and wonderful: I love you, Dad. And to Pat: thank you so much for the love and kindness and patience you have shown my father for all of these years. I am forever grateful for your presence in our lives.

I also have the best boyfriend in the world: Bill Weber, I love you, and thank you for being so supportive throughout this process, gently coaxing and cheering me along.

My kids are the best inspiration for everything I do, and I hope someday they can really appreciate how cool it is that Mom wrote a book.

And finally, to my mom in Heaven: I love you and miss you every day. I hope I make you proud. I wish you could be here to see this in person, because I wouldn't be here without your guidance throughout my life.

About the Author

Sarah Jones is a single working mother of three young children, who keep her incredibly busy. She hates doing dishes more than any other chore, so one-sheet-pan meals are her favorite. She has never particularly liked vegetables and loves sweets, but becoming a mom forced her to evaluate the way she was eating and make some changes, which is when she discovered keto. She currently resides in Jacksonville, Florida.

Index

Conversion Charts

Metric and Imperial Conversions

(These conversions are rounded for convenience)

Ingredient	Cups/ Tablespoons/ Teaspoons	Ounces	Grams/Milliliters
Butter	1 cup/ 16 tablespoons/ 2 sticks	8 ounces	230 grams
Cheese, shredded	1 cup	4 ounces	110 grams
Cream cheese	1 tablespoon	0.5 ounce	14.5 grams
Fruit, dried	1 cup	4 ounces	120 grams
Fruits or veggies, chopped	1 cup	5 to 7 ounces	145 to 200 grams
Fruits or veggies, pureed	1 cup	8.5 ounces	245 grams
Liquids: cream, milk, water, or juice	1 cup	8 fluid ounces	240 milliliters
Salt	1 teaspoon	0.2 ounce	6 grams
Spices: cinnamon, cloves, ginger, or nutmeg (ground)	1 teaspoon	0.2 ounce	5 milliliters
Vanilla extract	1 teaspoon	0.2 ounce	4 grams

Oven Temperatures

Fahrenheit	Celsius	Gas Mark
225°	110°	¼
250°	120°	½
275°	140°	1
300°	150°	2
325°	160°	3
350°	180°	4
375°	190°	5
400°	200°	6
425°	220°	7
450°	230°	8

Meal Planner

Week of: _____

	Breakfast	Lunch	Dinner
Saturday			
Friday			
Thursday			
Wednesday			
Tuesday			
Monday			
Sunday			

Meal Planner

Week of: _____

	Breakfast	Lunch	Dinner
Saturday			
Friday			
Thursday			
Wednesday			
Tuesday			
Monday			
Sunday			

Meal Planner

Week of: _____

	Breakfast	Lunch	Dinner
Saturday			
Friday			
Thursday			
Wednesday			
Tuesday			
Monday			
Sunday			

Meal Planner

Week of: _____

	Breakfast	Lunch	Dinner
Saturday			
Friday			
Thursday			
Wednesday			
Tuesday			
Monday			
Sunday			

Meal Planner

Week of: _____

	Breakfast	Lunch	Dinner
Saturday			
Friday			
Thursday			
Wednesday			
Tuesday			
Monday			
Sunday			

Meal Planner

Week of: _____

	Breakfast	Lunch	Dinner
Saturday			
Friday			
Thursday			
Wednesday			
Tuesday			
Monday			
Sunday			

Meal Planner

Week of: _____

	Breakfast	Lunch	Dinner
Saturday			
Friday			
Thursday			
Wednesday			
Tuesday			
Monday			
Sunday			

Meal Planner

Week of: _____

	Breakfast	Lunch	Dinner
Saturday			
Friday			
Thursday			
Wednesday			
Tuesday			
Monday			
Sunday			

Meal Planner

Week of: _____

	Breakfast	Lunch	Dinner
Saturday			
Friday			
Thursday			
Wednesday			
Tuesday			
Monday			
Sunday			

Meal Planner

Week of: _____

	Breakfast	Lunch	Dinner
Saturday			
Friday			
Thursday			
Wednesday			
Tuesday			
Monday			
Sunday			

Meal Planner

Week of: _____

	Breakfast	Lunch	Dinner
Saturday			
Friday			
Thursday			
Wednesday			
Tuesday			
Monday			
Sunday			

Meal Planner

Week of: _____

	Breakfast	Lunch	Dinner
Saturday			
Friday			
Thursday			
Wednesday			
Tuesday			
Monday			
Sunday			

Meal Planner

Week of: _____

	Breakfast	Lunch	Dinner
Saturday			
Friday			
Thursday			
Wednesday			
Tuesday			
Monday			
Sunday			

Meal Planner

Week of: _____

	Breakfast	Lunch	Dinner
Saturday			
Friday			
Thursday			
Wednesday			
Tuesday			
Monday			
Sunday			

Meal Planner

Week of: _____

	Breakfast	Lunch	Dinner
Saturday			
Friday			
Thursday			
Wednesday			
Tuesday			
Monday			
Sunday			

Meal Planner

Week of: _____

	Breakfast	Lunch	Dinner
Saturday			
Friday			
Thursday			
Wednesday			
Tuesday			
Monday			
Sunday			